Romances

1984

**National Library Service
for the Blind and
Physically Handicapped**

The Library of Congress

Please send your request
Lists to:
Braille Institute Library
741 No. Vermont
Los Angeles, CA 90029

Y0-CXN-023

Washington 1984

Library of Congress Cataloging in Publication Data
Main entry under title:

Romances.

  Includes index.
  Supt. of Docs. no.: LC 19.11:R66
  1. Blind, Books for the—Bibliography. 2. Talking
books—Bibliography. I. Library of Congress. National
Library Service for the Blind and Physically Handicapped.
Z5346.R65 1984 [HV1721]   016.80883′85   84-600112
ISBN 0-8444-0458-6

Contents

Introduction

This bibliography is a guide to selected romances. All books listed are available on disc, on cassette, or in braille in the network library collections provided by the National Library Service for the Blind and Physically Handicapped, Library of Congress.

Romances enjoyed wide readership in the eighteenth and early nineteenth centuries and resurged in demand in the early twentieth century. Their popularity today is attested by the fact that in this decade Barbara Cartland and Janet Dailey, prolific writers of romances, have become two of the world's five best-selling authors.

Most romance authors are women, and romances usually depict a woman's point of view. In a romance novel, the love story generally provides the major theme. Adventure or suspense may be present also, but those factors are secondary. Women's emotions, actions, and reactions are the elements of romances. A woman is usually at the center of the story, and her seeking for love, her relationship with a lover, and the resolution of her personal conflict inspire the story line.

Romances are written with happy endings, either fairy-tale or spicy. Heroines may be young, maidenly, experienced, or mature. Settings may be historical or contemporary, domestic or remote. While many romances in this bibliography depict artless, chaste heroines involved in sprightly adventures of love, others may feature protagonists whose romantic encounters may be characterized by explicit scenes of passion.

Romances issued by the publisher Harlequin are generally brief, with the plot revolving around the tortuous progress of the love relationship and its felicitous resolution. In *The Girl from Finlay's River*, by Elizabeth Graham, the heroine is in love with her employer, who is to marry someone else.

Regency romances such as those of Georgette Heyer are frilly tales set, usually in England, during the nineteenth-century regency of George, Prince of Wales. They may feature spirited women, sumptuous wardrobes, misunderstandings, and happy endings. They are often witty, peppered with period slang. Heyer's *Faro's Daughter* combines pretense and suspicion before heroine and hero declare their love.

A young woman in distress, a brooding, enigmatic hero, and an exotic or chilling setting may be components of a Gothic romance. In *The Mistress of Mellyn*, by Victoria Holt, a resourceful young woman protects a child, solves a mystery, escapes danger, and awakens the unhappy hero to her love—all against the backdrop of a Cornish manor.

A classic romance is one written before the twentieth century or a book widely read for a number of

Introduction

years. In Jane Austen's *Pride and Prejudice,* the romantic situations of five sisters are described, but it is the unconventional Elizabeth's experience with Mr. Darcy that captures the imagination.

Other romances range from the light-hearted *Any Two Can Play,* by Elizabeth Cadell, where Natalie encounters unlooked-for romance; to Laurie McBain's *Tears of Gold,* in which worldly-wise Mara in early California must endure a masquerade; to the innocent stories of Barbara Cartland, such as *Love Locked In,* where the duke is sophisticated and jaded, while the country lass is ingenuous and honorable.

This bibliography is available in large-print, disc, and braille formats. The large-print edition contains more than 700 titles on disc, on cassette, or in braille. The disc edition lists only recorded materials; the braille edition lists only braille. In the large-print and disc editions, books available on flexible-disc are cited with their cassette versions.

Each book is described briefly. The list is divided into five subject sections. Within each section, disc books, cassette books, and braille books appear in succession arranged alphabetically by author. The alphabetical author-title indexes at the end of the list are also grouped according to disc, cassette, or braille format.

To order books, fill out the order form at the back of the bibliography and send it to your cooperating library. Book numbers are listed by media. Flexible-disc book numbers are included on the order form following the braille listing.

Harlequin Romances

Discs

They Came to Valeira   RD 14138
by Rosalind Brett
narrated by Michael Clarke-Laurence
3 discs
Plantation manager Julian Caswell becomes angry when he discovers Philippa Crane on Valeira. He had hoped for solitude and complete relief from women on the tropical island, and commands her to leave. But plucky Philippa is determined to remain, especially when she discovers that she has fallen in love with the wary Julian. 1974.

Enchanted Woods   RD 20273
by Katrina Britt
narrated by Patricia Kilgarriff
3 discs
Raised in an orphanage, Sally has always longed for a home and family. At twenty-five, the young nurse has three fine candidates for a husband, any one of whom would fit her careful plans. She has not, however, counted on the disturbing presence of a handsome brain surgeon who turns the head of every woman he meets. 1978.

The Awakening   RD 19048
by Rosemary Carter
narrated by Michael McCullough
2 discs
After her parents' deaths, Robyne Sloan has to fight to keep her family together and make a living from the dry African soil. Then, when she thinks that life can get no harder,

businessman Dean Mornay decides to foreclose their mortgage. 1979.

The Gift of Love   RD 19015
by Margaret Chapman
narrated by Madelyn Buzzard
2 discs
Francesca had been happy while her mother was alive and housekeeper at Old Beams. But everything is different now that Francesca seeks the job as housekeeper to the new owner, the famous composer and concert pianist, Adam Greco. And even worse, she has fallen in love with him. 1977.

The Island Bride   RD 19331
by Jane Corrie
narrated by Jack Fox
2 discs
Cara's joyous return to French Polynesia is ruined when she runs into the man to whom she was married by an island chieftain in a primitive ceremony six years ago. Neither Cara nor Pierre Morelon, the island's most influential man, have seen one another since their peculiar wedding, and Cara wants to keep it that way. 1978.

Prince of Darkness   RD 18232
by Susanna Firth
narrated by Michael McCullough
2 discs
Cassandra made the painful decision to leave her husband, Elliott, when his business became more important than their marriage. For five years she has kept busy selling real estate in

France, when Elliott suddenly turns up as her new boss. 1979.

**The Girl from Finlay's River
RD 19829**
by Elizabeth Graham
narrated by Becky Parker
2 discs
Fresh from her family's prairie farm in Saskatchewan, Mairi falls in love with the beautiful coastal city of Vancouver. She soon falls in love with her boss, too, and regrets it because he has already chosen beautiful Naomi Prentiss, daughter of one of Vancouver's wealthiest families, to be his bride. 1976.

Harbour of Love   RD 19008
by Anne Hampson
narrated by Michael McCullough
2 discs
Liane loved Richard Wilding for six years, but he saw her only as his efficient, self-effacing secretary. When he becomes engaged to another woman, she takes a holiday to visit her cousin in South Africa and sort out her tangled emotions. Liane had thought she could never love another man, but in meeting Flind Dawson she experiences some doubts. 1977.

Prisoner of the Harem   RD 19049
by Julia Herbert
narrated by Bruce Huntey
2 discs
In Naples with her archaeologist uncle, Felicity is attracted to Andre, a suave Frenchman, while her cousin

Rosanna is in love with an Italian. When the girls are kidnapped by an Algerian corsair and held prisoner in a harem, the heartbroken Felicity is convinced that Andre has betrayed them. 1978.

Stranger at the Gate   RD 19514
by Frances Lang
narrated by Jack Fox
2 discs
Set in seventeenth-century France during a time of religious persecution, this novel follows the love affair between a beautiful Huguenot woman and a dashing count who is faithful to the King's religion. 1975.

Dangerous Enchantment   RD 14136
by Anne Mather
narrated by Tom Martin
2 discs
Julie Kennedy has worshipped singer Manuel Cortez from afar, and she can't believe her luck when he shows an interest in her. Julie's head tells her that she is just another woman to him, but her heart won't let go. 1969.

Love's Puppet   RD 19848
by Henrietta Reid
narrated by Mitzi Friedlander
3 discs
Marc has no intention of marrying the girl his mother picked out for him. To defy his mother, he persuades little Ella Benson, who is mourning her lost lover, to pose as his fiancée at a grand engagement ball. 1975.

Stranger's Kiss   RD 20276
by Sondra Stanford
narrated by Aviva Skell
2 discs
Darcy astounds herself by agreeing to a marriage of convenience with a handsome stranger, a rich Texas rancher who saved her life. She accepts the arrangement at face value until the appearance of one of Mike's old girl friends forces her to admit that she loves him. 1978.

Other Woman   RD 19816
by Jessica Steele
narrated by Michael McCullough
2 discs
Georgina's handsome new boss becomes convinced she is having an affair with co-worker Desmond Warner. Despite her protests that their relationship is platonic, her arrogant employer threatens to fire her. 1980.

Blue Lotus   RD 20270
by Margaret Way
narrated by Michael McCullough
2 discs
Lost in the treacherous rain forest of Queensland, Australia, Susan is rescued by Devin Chandler, who takes her to his private kingdom. His jealous, widowed sister-in-law makes life difficult for lovely Susan, who is both afraid of Devin and strongly attracted to him. 1979.

White Magnolia   RD 20285
by Margaret Way
narrated by Hillary Ryan Norton
2 discs
Grief-stricken and guilty over the sudden death of her ex-fiancé, Nicole needs time to heal. Her recuperation is cut short by Quinn Rossiter, manager of a sprawling Australian cattle farm. Nicole promises herself to stay away from him, but she is attracted by the violent excitement he arouses in her. 1979.

Dangerous Marriage   RD 18717
by Mary Wibberley
narrated by Sherry Kendell
2 discs
When Shelley's domineering father sends her to the island of Avala to buy a hotel, she rejoices in her new independence. However, the handsome island entrepreneur reveals that her father is plotting to keep her under his thumb. 1980.

Witchwood   RD 20269
by Mary Wibberley
narrated by Michael McCullough
2 discs
Beth is traveling from London to meet the grandfather she has never seen when a snowstorm strands her in an abandoned cottage with a total stranger. A handsome, hostile man who knows her grandfather well, he doubts that Beth is really related to the wealthy old man who is recovering from heart surgery. The stranger suggests that the only way for Beth to

avoid shocking her grandfather to death is to arrive with him as his wife. 1978.

The Honey Is Bitter   RD 19314
by Violet Winspear
narrated by Michael McCullough
2 discs
A wealthy Greek shipping-line owner demands payment when one of Domini's relatives forges checks with his signature. To save the family's reputation, she agrees to a loveless marriage with the enigmatic tycoon, who keeps her a virtual prisoner on a Greek island. 1967.

The Strange Waif   RD 14086
by Violet Winspear
narrated by Michael McCullough
1 disc
Dr. Avery Chase is smitten with the girl he finds huddled on his doorstep and suffering from amnesia. Avery's cynical cousin Bob, a dashing actor, believes the girl is faking, yet he is strangely attracted to her. The sole clue to the girl's identity is the mark of a ring on the third finger of her left hand. 1962.

Cassettes

Love This Stranger   RC 14300
by Rosalind Brett
narrated by Janis Gray
2 cassettes
Nineteen-year-old Tess Bentley single-handedly runs a general store in the

middle of the African veld. Despite her protests, a young man arranges to take the store out of her hands and ruthlessly organizes her life. 1966.

Bush Doctor   RC 13836
by Rosemary Carter
narrated by Nancy Loucks
1 cassette
Stacey accepts a nursing assignment in a remote hospital near the African jungle. She is astonished to discover that one of the doctors at the hospital is a former lover she is desperately trying to forget. Also issued on flexible disc as FD 13836. 1979.

Sweet Impostor   RC 13821
by Rosemary Carter
narrated by Mitzi Friedlander
1 cassette
Follows the fortunes of Roumayne, who has been unjustly accused of causing a popular singer's death. Fired from her job, jilted by her fiance, and damned by public opinion, she eagerly accepts an offer to go to South Africa and impersonate her friend. Also issued on flexible disc as FD 13821. 1979.

The Bride of the Delta Queen
RC 14305
by Janet Dailey
narrated by Norman Barrs
2 cassettes
Selena is vacationing alone in New Orleans. Although she successfully resists the insistent advances of the men she meets, she finds danger when she

accepts an invitation from a woman to cruise aboard the riverboat, the Delta Queen. 1978.

Dear Plutocrat   RC 20187
by Anne Hampson
narrated by Azaleigh Maginnis
1 cassette
When Kate Beresford inherits some property from a distant relative in the Australian outback, she and two friends decide to settle there. Upon arriving, she finds her neighbor Mark Copeland is eager to buy her holding. Kate holds firm, but falls in love with Mark in the process. 1976.

Bargain Bride   RC 20410
by Flora Kidd
narrated by Charlotte Stanton
1 cassette
Lee travels to Curacao to marry Adrian, only to find that he has left the island. Within the hour, though, she receives a marriage proposal from his very practical former employer. 1979.

The Devil's Arms   RC 14282
by Charlotte Lamb
narrated by Michael McCullough
1 cassette
A young woman awakens on a lonely moor with no recollection of who she is or where she has been. Although her rescuer, a painter, insists he knows her identity and that they are engaged, the amnesia victim has grave

doubts that she is the flirtatious, unscrupulous woman he reveals to her. Some strong language. 1978.

Chase a Green Shadow   RC 14306
by Anne Mather
narrated by Michael McCullough
1 cassette
Tamsyn reluctantly goes to visit her father in Wales. There she meets an older man who arouses powerful, conflicting emotions within her. 1973.

Fallen Angel   RC 14283
by Anne Mather
narrated by Janis Gray
2 cassettes
A sophisticated Englishman is astonished to discover that he has become the guardian of an affection-starved teenager brought up in a French convent. He reluctantly agrees to take his insistent young ward to his South American ranch. Some strong language. 1978.

Legacy of the Past   RC 15016
by Anne Mather
narrated by Tom Martin
1 cassette
There have been two men so far in Madeline's life—her late husband Joe and her boss Adrian. Both have been kind and uncomplicated, wanting only to cherish and care for her. Then she falls madly in love with Nicholas Vitale—dynamic, rich, irresistible, and used to having his own way. 1966.

Harlequin Romances Cassettes

Leopard in the Snow   RC 12949
by Anne Mather
narrated by Connie Meng
1 cassette
A young woman rebels against her father and leaves for London. Lost in a blizzard, she is forced to accept the help of a terse, uncommunicative young man whom she learns to resent and also to love. Also issued on flexible disc as FD 12949. 1974.

The Night of the Bulls   RC 14303
by Anne Mather
narrated by Michael McCullough
1 cassette
In a remote area in the south of france, Dionne returns to seek help from her ex-lover, who does not know he is the father of her child. Reviving memories of their tragic and passionate affair three years ago, the journey forces her to examine her own feelings for her lover and to confront the opposition of his mother. 1972.

Prelude to Enchantment   RC 14373
by Anne Mather
narrated by Dale Carter
1 cassette
On assignment to interview a famous author at his palazzo in Venice, a reporter falls in love with him. When she learns he desperately needs money and that a glamorous, wealthy woman is ready to marry him, she despairs of ever finding a place in his heart. 1972.

A Savage Beauty   RC 16296
by Anne Mather
narrated by Mimi Bederman
1 cassette
Most women would envy Emma Seaton. She is comfortably, if not excitingly, engaged to a business tycoon who can give her a life of luxury and ease. Then Miguel sweeps into her life, and she knows without doubt that she has never loved any other man. 1973.

Champagne Spring   RC 18571
by Margaret Rome
narrated by Kerry Cundiff
1 cassette
Chantal and her brother can hardly believe their luck when they inherit prosperous vineyards in France. However, their arrogant, sophisticated neighbor, Marquis de la Roque, scoffs at their plans to work the land themselves. 1979.

Apollo's Daughter   RC 19482
by Rebecca Stratton
narrated by Michael McCullough
2 cassettes
Bethany's life on a Greek island is carefree until stern Nikolas becomes her guardian. At first she is repulsed by his determination to turn her into the traditional Greek lady, but she soon finds herself behaving very seductively toward him. 1980.

Goddess of Mavisu   RC 19571
by Rebecca Stratton
narrated by Jack Fox
1 cassette
Delia knew she should never have let herself fall in love with the devastating Kemal Selin. He is a Turk who wants a meek and docile wife of his own nationality. But as Delia knows too well, feelings are difficult to control. 1976.

The Glass Castle   RC 15916
by Violet Winspear
narrated by Gerry Kasarda
1 cassette
Edwin Trequair, a mysterious and very rich entrepreneur, asks Heron Brooks to marry him, and she accepts. Worldly Edwin has his own reasons for proposing to her, but Heron doesn't know why she agrees to marry a brooding Cornishman whom she dares not love. 1973.

The Valdez Marriage   RC 14374
by Violet Winspear
narrated by Michael McCullough
1 cassette
Darcy feels guilty when Ramon, a music student from Spain, is left paralyzed after an automobile accident in her car. Ramon's arrogant brother summons Darcy to his Spanish estate and expects her to marry Ramon, whom she does not love. 1978.

Braille

Love This Stranger   BR 4209
by Rosalind Brett
2 volumes
Nineteen-year-old Tess Bentley single-handedly runs a general store in the middle of the African veld. Despite her protests, a young man arranges to take the store out of her hands and ruthlessly organizes her life. 1966.

Bush Doctor   BR 4189
by Rosemary Carter
2 volumes
Stacey accepts a nursing assignment in a remote hospital near the African jungle. She is astonished to discover that one of the doctors at the hospital is a former lover she is desperately trying to forget. 1979.

For Love of a Pagan   BR 5362
by Anne Hampson
2 volumes
Tina is both incensed and amused when Paul, a Greek tycoon and playboy, asks her to become his mistress. Knowing that she is far from indifferent to him, Tina returns home to England. But when Paul follows and proposes to her, she is faced with an entirely different kind of decision. 1978.

Harlequin Romances

The Devil's Arms   BR 4210
by Charlotte Lamb
2 volumes
A young woman awakens on a lonely moor with no recollection of who she is or where she has been. Although her rescuer, a painter, insists he knows her identity and that they are engaged, the amnesia victim has grave doubts that she is the flirtatious, unscrupulous woman he reveals to her. Some strong language. 1978.

Bitter Homecoming   BR 5638
by Jan MacLean
2 volumes
The bitter, withdrawn man who returns to Sevenoaks is not the man Kate knew and loved. Of course, his wife's death would have been traumatic, but Adam refuses to speak about it. While Kate hopes her love for Adam will still the ghost of his past, he gives her no chance at all. 1978.

Vanishing Bride   BR 5232
by Magali
2 volumes
Fate saves Marion from a deadly plane crash, giving her the chance to begin her life over again in remote Sardinia. But her momentary calm is shattered by the intrigue and trickery that permeate the ancient walls of Castel Terralba. 1977.

Chase a Green Shadow   BR 4199
by Anne Mather
2 volumes
Tamsyn reluctantly goes to visit her father in Wales. There she meets an older man who arouses powerful, conflicting emotions within her. 1973.

Dangerous Enchantment   BR 4430
by Anne Mather
2 volumes
Julie Kennedy has worshipped singer Manuel Cortez from afar, and she can't believe her luck when he shows an interest in her. Julie's head tells her that she is just another woman to him, but her heart won't let go. 1969.

Legacy of the Past   BR 4441
by Anne Mather
2 volumes
There have been two men so far in Madeline's life—her late husband Joe and her boss Adrian. Both have been kind and uncomplicated, wanting only to cherish and care for her. Then she falls madly in love with Nicholas Vitale—dynamic, rich, irresistible, and used to having his own way. 1966.

The Night of the Bulls   BR 4212
by Anne Mather
1 volume
In a remote area in the south of France, Dionne returns to seek help from her ex-lover, who does not know he is the father of her child. Reviving memories of their tragic and passionate affair three years ago, the journey forces her to examine her own feel-

ings for her lover and to confront the opposition of his mother. 1972.

Prelude to Enchantment   BR 4208
by Anne Mather
2 volumes
On assignment to interview a famous author at his palazzo in Venice, a reporter falls in love with him. When she learns he desperately needs money and that a glamorous, wealthy woman is ready to marry him, she despairs of ever finding a place in his heart. 1972.

A Savage Beauty   BR 4425
by Anne Mather
2 volumes
Most women would envy Emma Seaton. She is comfortably, if not excitingly, engaged to a business tycoon who can give her a life of luxury and ease. Then Miguel sweeps into her life, and she knows without doubt that she has never loved any other man. 1973.

Marriage Impossible   BR 5646
by Margaret Pargeter
2 volumes
Tanga's life on a beautiful South Pacific island had been idyllic until her father died. When her arrogant neighbor high-handedly takes charge of her, she resents his treating her like a child, especially since she finds him so attractive. 1978.

Bitter Alliance   BR 5413
by Kay Thorpe
2 volumes
It is true that it only took Jaime two short weeks to fall out of love with Tristan Caine and into love with his formidable older brother, Liam. But she is not the cheap little gold digger he thinks her, and somehow she just has to prove he is wrong. 1979.

Garden of Thorns   BR 5207
by Sally Wentworth
2 volumes
Kirsty, recently moved from a comfortable London apartment to a tumbledown country cottage of her own, finds herself falling headlong in love with the aristocratic local squire, who wants to drive her from the neighborhood. 1980.

Say Hello to Yesterday   BR 5392
by Sally Wentworth
2 volumes
Holly Weston had done it all alone. She had raised her small son and worked her way up to features writer for a major newspaper after her husband Nick Falconer left her. She thought it was over and done with until an assignment in Greece brought her face to face with Nick and all she was trying to forget. 1981.

A Dangerous Man   BR 5639
by Mary Wibberley
2 volumes
Everyone in the Yorkshire village where Tania teaches school expects

9

her to marry Ted Latham, the spoiled son of a rich builder. But everything changes when fearless Bryden Kane arrives in Granchester to challenge Tania's prospective father-in-law. 1979.

Dearest Demon   BR 5338
by Violet Winspear
2 volumes
Destine's life seemed to stop with the death of her doctor-husband on their wedding day two years ago. Knowing that she cannot continue to live in the past, Destine takes a position in Spain as a nurse and is reawakened emotionally by the handsome, passionate Don Artez. 1976.

The Valdez Marriage   BR 4207
by Violet Winspear
2 volumes
Darcy feels guilty when Ramon, a music student from Spain, is left paralyzed after an automobile accident in her car. Ramon's arrogant brother summons Darcy to his Spanish estate and expects her to marry Ramon, whom she does not love. 1978.

Regency Romances

Discs

The Smile of the Stranger   RD 13141
by Joan Aiken
narrated by Mitzi Friedlander
4 discs
Juliana Paget and her dying father, an expatriate writer living in Italy, are forced to return to the ancestral mansion in Regency England. Once there, Juliana must contend with troublesome relatives, worthless suitors, and murderous assaults until she finds her true love. 1978.

The Emerald Necklace   RD 15630
by Diana Brown
narrated by Mitzi Friedlander
4 discs
In Regency London, proud young Lady Leonora Fordyce, the daughter of a peer, marries Etienne Lambert, a self-made man of illegitimate birth, to free her father from his gambling debts. In marriage, Leonora begins to change from a vain woman into a self-reliant one, and Etienne's honest generosity reveals his true feelings for his wife. 1980.

Marsanne   RD 10622
by Virginia Coffman
narrated by Dale Carter
3 discs
Elegant Regency England is contrasted with the turbulence of France on the eve of Napoleon Bonaparte's return from Elba. Marsanne is dispatched to the presumed safety of Royalist relatives in England, where

she falls in love with Sir Philip Justin. His secret connection with smugglers, pirates, and political events thrusts the young heiress into dangerous cross-currents of intrigue, deceit, and high romance. 1976.

Allegra   RD 8381
by Clare Darcy
narrated by Dale Carter
3 discs
Convinced that her cousin's proposal of marriage on the death of her father springs from pity, Allegra leaves for Brussels with her sister Hilary. There the girls become unwitting dupes in the war against Napoleon and appeal to the cousin for rescue. 1974.

Cressida   RD 10948
by Clare Darcy
narrated by Mitzi Friedlander
3 discs
A socialite's world is turned around when a lover who jilted her returns after six years of far-flung adventures. 1977.

Gwendolen   RD 13132
by Clare Darcy
narrated by Dale Carter
2 discs
In Regency England's frivolous society, rich, brusque Marquis Lyndale and Gwendolen "come to cuffs" instantly when he seeks the hand of her sister, Jane. Jane loves a poor young man but feels bound to accept Lyndale to save the family estate. Cir-

Regency Romances Discs

cumstances, however, intervene to avert future complications. 1978.

Lady Pamela   RD 11557
by Clare Darcy
narrated by Christina Gillespie
3 discs
In Regency England headstrong Lady Pamela Frayne flouts conventions, which worries her powerful grandfather. She becomes an irresistible challenge to a nobleman who had known only easy conquests in love until he met her. 1975.

April Lady   RD 10232
by Georgette Heyer
narrated by Adale O'Brien
3 discs
Lady Helen gets into trouble by telling little white lies in an effort to help such deserving people as her dashing, debt-ridden brother and her husband's lovesick young sister. One fib too many puts her marriage in jeopardy. 1957.

Bath Tangle   RD 15685
by Georgette Heyer
narrated by Michael McCullough
4 discs
Lady Serena Carlow raged as she heard her father's last will and testament—how could he mortgage his only daughter to the odious Lord Ivo Rotherham, making the very man she had recently jilted caretaker of her inheritance and her heart? 1955.

The Corinthian   RD 10951
by Georgette Heyer
narrated by Michael McCullough
3 discs
Penelope Creed escapes from entering a hated marriage by joining Sir Richard Wyndham on his flight from a beautiful, but dull, young lady his family wants him to marry. 1974.

Cotillion   RD 6313
by Georgette Heyer
narrated by Mitzi Friedlander
5 discs
In Regency England, a young ward of a stingy old gentleman pretends to agree with her guardian's plans for her marriage, but she eventually succeeds in having her own way. 1953.

Faro's Daughter   RD 9973
by Georgette Heyer
narrated by Terry Hayes Sales
4 discs
A young woman who runs a Faro table in her aristocratic aunt's London gaming house is wooed by young Lord Mablethorp and his more mature cousin Ravenscar. 1942.

The Grand Sophy   RD 9965
by Georgette Heyer
narrated by Rachel Gurney
4 discs
Madcap tale set in the Regency days in London with an irresistible heroine almost six-feet tall. Because of her forthright manner and ingenious matchmaking and organizing ability,

12

Sophy becomes a smashing success. 1950.

Lady of Quality   RD 10528
by Georgette Heyer
narrated by Rachel Gurney
3 discs
Annis Wychwood, twenty-nine, is regarded as a hopeless spinster by all Bath society. 1972.

Regency Buck   RD 11201
by Georgette Heyer
narrated by Meg Wynn-Owen
4 discs
Miss Traverner, a young Regency England heiress, and her brother Peregrine travel from Yorkshire to London to meet their guardian. A number of surprising events occur: someone tries to poison Peregrine, and Miss Traverner's guardian turns away her suitors. 1935.

Venetia   RD 6867
by Georgette Heyer
narrated by Terry Hayes Sales
5 discs
Venetia manages the family estate and takes care of her younger brother, who is lame, while her older brother is with the army occupying Europe after the battle of Waterloo. Lord Damerel, a dashing rake, is but one of the many suitors who pursues Venetia. 1973.

Marry in Haste   RD 11640
by Jane Aiken Hodge
narrated by Pat Gilbert-Read
3 discs
Adventure novel set in Regency England and Portugal. After agreeing to a marriage in name only, a young French refugee falls in love with her enigmatic English husband. When he is sent to Lisbon on a diplomatic mission, she discovers that he is really a spy. 1969.

Eccentric Lady   RD 19837
by Jane Lovelace
narrated by Tom Martin
2 discs
Lady Elizabeth would rather feed her chickens and breed horses on her farms than join the London party-goers in search of a husband. But Beth's uncle, Lord Farling, lays down the law: if she wants to maintain control of the estate, she must partake of one social season. She agrees to the bargain, but clever Beth has a plan. 1983.

Earl and the Heiress   RD 19818
by Barbara Metzger
narrated by Becky Parker
3 discs
An inherited town house carries Noelle Armstrong, an impoverished young woman, and her brother and sister to the fringes of society. Their assets include intelligence, beauty, the brother's title, and five exotic little dogs that take London by storm. The dogs also introduce Noelle to a rakish

earl, who buys a puppy for his mistress while doggedly pursuing Noelle. 1982.

Dame Durden's Daughter   RD 13121
by Joan Smith
narrated by Tom Martin
2 discs
The Duke of Saymore has the reputation of a rake. On his return from the Continent to his sleepy village, he finds perky Eddie Durden, once his youthful companion, has turned into a young woman. Pitfalls and misunderstandings temporarily mar their romance. 1978.

Imprudent Lady   RD 18276
by Joan Smith
narrated by Michael McCullough
3 discs
Prudence Mallow, a young writer, becomes the toast of Regency London when her successful novels bring her into public view and into the heart of the town's dashing poet laureate. 1978.

Some Brief Folly   RD 17524
by Patricia Veryan
narrated by Michael McCullough
4 discs
A landslide near Bath introduces a London woman to the infamous Garret Hawkhurst, a dangerous libertine said to have caused the deaths of his own wife and child. 1981.

Quicksilver Lady   RD 15165
by Barbara Whitehead
narrated by Mitzi Friedlander
4 discs
In Regency England, restless, headstrong Arabella goes husband-hunting. She tastes the delights of the London social season, arranges love matches for her friends, and gets into various entanglements with young men. 1979.

Cassettes

The Five-Minute Marriage   RC 15193
by Joan Aiken
narrated by Ann Pugh
2 cassettes
Delphie Carteret, struggling to support herself and her mother, discovers that an imposter has been taking both her place and a large inheritance set aside for her. In order to claim them, Delphie reluctantly agrees to a counterfeit marriage to her cousin Gareth. 1977.

Come Be My Love   RC 18482
by Diana Brown
narrated by Michael McCullough
2 cassettes
Hopelessly in love with the heir of a nearby estate, the liberated Alexandra becomes a famous writer and the toast of London. Some descriptions of sex. 1981.

Riding to the Moon RC 19352
by Barbara Cartland
narrated by Michael McCullough
1 cassette
A wager over whether a gentleman can marry only someone blue-blooded brings a wealthy tradesman's daughter, Indira Rowlandson, and the Marquis of Ardsley together under bizarre, then more romantic, circumstances. 1982.

Minerva RC 19782
by Marion Chesney
narrated by Mitzi Friedlander
2 cassettes
Minerva, the oldest of six marriageable sisters and two brothers, children of an impoverished vicar, is elected by her father to rescue the family fortune. His best bet is to send the beautiful but prudish Minerva to London for the season in the hope that she will land a rich husband. Some descriptions of sex. 1983.

The Tynedale Daughters RC 18527
by Norma Lee Clark
narrated by Grace Ragsdale
2 cassettes
A frothy period piece set in Regency England. Two of the three Tynedale daughters are engaged, but each falls in love with the other's fiance. The third and youngest daughter both loves and hates the distant cousin who will inherit their estate unless the three sisters produce sons. 1981.

Sara RC 16274
by Brian Cleeve
narrated by Grace Ragsdale
3 cassettes
Destiny casts a Spanish orphan into the snares and seductions of Regency London, where she is pounced upon by bold men who love her to the edge of obsession and beyond. Some strong language. 1976.

Cecily; Or, A Young Lady of Quality RC 9608
by Clare Darcy
narrated by Jane Winther
3 cassettes
Relates a young woman's stage career in Regency England and her encounter with a distant cousin. 1972.

Eugenia RC 12887
by Clare Darcy
narrated by Mitzi Friedlander
2 cassettes
Headstrong Eugenia Liddiard, ready for her first season in Regency London, rescues from the Bow Street Runners a long-lost cousin suspected of murder. After many chases and narrow escapes, the lively young heroine is able to win her true love. 1977.

Lydia; Or, Love in Town RC 9862
by Clare Darcy
narrated by Patricia Leclercq
2 cassettes
An impetuous young woman from Louisiana arrives in Regency London with her family at the height of the season and announces her intention to

marry for wealth and position. She keeps two eligible bachelors at a distance while she defies an arrogant aristocrat. 1973.

Regina   RC 10614
by Clare Darcy
narrated by Terry Hayes Sales
2 cassettes
An elegant young widow in Regency England meets the sardonic Lord Wrexam and realizes she will have difficulty trying to keep her seventeen-year-old cousin from marrying him. 1976.

Victoire   RC 8550
by Clare Darcy
narrated by Patricia Beaudry
4 cassettes
Innocent young Victoire is forced by her uncle to participate in the blackmail of Lord Tarn. Tarn is kidnapped and then rescued by Victoire. 1974.

A Suitable Match   RC 16665
by Joy Freeman
narrated by Rachel Gurney
2 cassettes
A Regency romance featuring a pair of lovers in each other's arms and at each other's throats. A beautiful girl with good sense seems doomed to spinsterhood as long as she is courted by a rakish earl sworn to bachelorhood—though not to celibacy. 1980.

Black Sheep   RC 11598
by Georgette Heyer
narrated by Virginia Cromer
2 cassettes
A seemingly sedate lady of twenty-eight decides to save a young niece from a fortune hunter but falls victim to the young man's black-sheep uncle. 1966.

A Civil Contract   RC 10413
by Georgette Heyer
narrated by Norman Barrs
3 cassettes
Charming tale of Regency England concerns a marriage of convenience between impoverished Captain Adam Deveril, once an officer with the Duke of Wellington, and Jenny Chawleigh, an heiress. 1971.

The Convenient Marriage   RC 10847
by Georgette Heyer
narrated by Diane Eilenberg
2 cassettes
When a self-possessed young woman marries a powerful earl, she believes she is rescuing her sister from a loveless match and restoring her family fortunes. Afterwards she finds that she is in love with her husband. Also issued on flexible disc as FD 10847. 1966.

Cousin Kate   RC 13368
by Georgette Heyer
narrated by Meg Wynn-Owen
2 cassettes
Kate, an orphaned and penniless young lady, is befriended by an un-

known aunt and installed in luxury at Staplewood. She begins to suspect that her aunt's kindness cloaks a cruel plan, and finds that she is the intended bride of her handsome but mad young cousin. 1968.

The Foundling   RC 13281
by Georgette Heyer
narrated by Hal Tenny
3 cassettes
A sheltered, disenchanted young duke eludes his protectors and sets out to enjoy the robust life of Regency England. He encounters many experiences he had not bargained for and is involved with a serene woman who becomes the decoy for a ruthless blackmailer. 1977.

An Infamous Army   RC 11837
by Georgette Heyer
narrated by Ruth Stokesberry
3 cassettes
On the eve of the Battle of Waterloo, a flirtatious widow shocks everyone in Brussels by promising to marry a dashing young colonel on the Duke of Wellington's staff. 1965.

The Nonesuch   RC 18185
by Georgette Heyer
narrated by Tom Martin
2 cassettes
The most talked-about bachelor in London society inherits a Yorkshire estate. The legacy changes his life and leads him to a most surprising choice of a bride. 1962.

Sprig Muslin   RC 10357
by Georgette Heyer
narrated by Flo Gibson
2 cassettes
Willful, flirtatious Amanda runs away from her doting grandfather, who objects to her engagement to an impoverished young officer. A dashing older man crosses her path and becomes an unwilling protector. 1972.

**Sylvester; Or, The Wicked Uncle
RC 11652**
by Georgette Heyer
narrated by Meg Wynn-Owen
2 cassettes
Set in Regency England, this romantic tale is about a wealthy, arrogant, and handsome duke and the only girl in the whole country who seems to dislike him. 1957.

These Old Shades   RC 16675
by Georgette Heyer
narrated by Flo Gibson
2 cassettes
The Duke of Avon rescues a young French waif from the clutches of a brutal relative and takes the lad to become his page, without realizing the boy is really a girl. 1966.

The Toll-Gate   RC 10760
by Georgette Heyer
narrated by Ken Meeker
2 cassettes
After the glory of Waterloo, a young captain of the dragoons leaves the army to escape boredom and is imme-

diately plunged into more exciting hazards than he anticipated. 1954.

The Stanbroke Girls   RC 17841
by Fiona Hill
narrated by Laura Giannarelli
2 cassettes
Romance, wit, and nineteenth-century high style accompany the Stanbroke girls—impulsive Lady Isabella and her young sister, Lady Elizabeth. Elizabeth is mad for a detestable rake, while Isabella seems a perfect match for a very eligible bachelor who is as unattainable as he is desirable. 1981.

Sweet's Folly   RC 10566
by Fiona Hill
narrated by Patricia Beaudry
2 cassettes
Bright, lively Regency tale involves orphaned Honoria Newcombe who, raised by two unworldly aunts, decides not to be a burden to them any longer and marries an unresponsive husband. 1977.

Rebel Heiress   RC 11461
by Jane Aiken Hodge
narrated by Patricia Beaudry
2 cassettes
On the eve of the War of 1812, Henrietta Marchmont, a bold Yankee woman from Boston, sails to London to claim her rightful place in her father's family, the powerful Marchmont dynasty. She encounters unexpected complications of head and heart. 1975.

The Day of the Butterfly   RC 14066
by Norah Lofts
narrated by Yvonne Fair Tessler
3 cassettes
When Daisy Holt is fired from her first job as a nursemaid, her luck goes from bad to worse, and she seems destined for a life in a London brothel. But her radiance attracts the eye of an artist, and Daisy experiences her first romance and the first of her sorrows as well. Also issued on flexible disc as FD 14066. 1979.

The Caretaker Wife   RC 12365
by Barbara Whitehead
narrated by Gerry Kasarda
2 cassettes
In Regency England shy, unmarried, thirty-year-old Caroline accepts a proposal of marriage from a widower who needs a mother for his five children. When the lieutenant goes off to war for three years, she copes with the children and a malevolent nursemaid and develops a crush on an Italian footman. 1977.

Braille

The Smile of the Stranger   BR 4177
by Joan Aiken
4 volumes
Juliana Paget and her dying father, an expatriate writer living in Italy, are forced to return to the ancestral mansion in Regency England. Once there Juliana must contend with troublesome relatives, worthless suitors, and

murderous assaults until she finds her true love. 1978.

Regency Rogue   BR 5272
by Helen Ashfield
2 volumes
When Lady Davina Temple and the Earl of Dunmorrow meet at a house party, each is engaged to someone else and both dread their approaching marriages. The disappearance of their host turns the earl to sleuthing. Davina is distressed however to discover a few clues that point to the earl himself. 1982.

The Tynedale Daughters   BR 4954
by Norma Lee Clark
2 volumes
A frothy period piece set in Regency England. Two of the three Tynedale daughters are engaged, but each falls in love with the other's fiance. The third and youngest daughter both loves and hates the distant cousin who will inherit their estate unless the three sisters produce sons. 1981.

See No Love   BR 5664
by Monette Cummings
2 volumes
A matchmaking mother is fervently convinced that the sight of her daughter in spectacles would frighten off any suitor. Thus Emily becomes involved in a series of minor disasters until she is rescued by a duke who encourages her to wear eyeglasses. 1983.

Eugenia   BR 3424
by Clare Darcy
2 volumes
Headstrong Eugenia Liddiard, ready for her first season in Regency London, rescues from the Bow Street Runners a long-lost cousin who is suspected of murder. After many chases and narrow escapes, the lively young heroine is able to win her true love. 1977.

Letty   BR 4515
by Clare Darcy
2 volumes
Headstrong Letty Montressor runs away from an arranged marriage in Regency London and literally bumps into rakish Harry Tyne, disowned great-nephew of rich Lord Aubrey. Harry discovers that Letty has a beautiful voice and whisks her off to Vienna to be the singing star of his new gambling salon, where she promptly falls in love with him. 1980.

A Suitable Match   BR 4811
by Joy Freeman
4 volumes
A Regency romance featuring a pair of lovers in each other's arms and at each other's throats. A beautiful girl with good sense seems doomed to spinsterhood as long as she is courted by a rakish earl sworn to bachelorhood—though not to celibacy. 1980.

Lovers Meeting BR 4220
by Mollie Hardwick
3 volumes
Historical romance set in the theater
world of Regency England blends the
lives of four fellow players in panto-
mime. They are the beautiful Cockney dancer Jannie; the gifted and
ambitious Welshman Ivor; the lonely
aging actress Sara; and Raymond, a
once notable tragic actor with a past
to conceal. 1979.

Arabella BR 2069
by Georgette Heyer
5 volumes
When the daughter of a country parson is sent to London to make a good
marriage, she poses as an heiress and
becomes the talk of the town and the
catch of the season. 1966.

Cousin Kate BR 988
by Georgette Heyer
4 volumes
Kate, an orphaned and penniless
young lady, is befriended by an unknown aunt and installed in luxury at
Staplewood. She begins to suspect
that her aunt's kindness cloaks a cruel
plan and finds that she is the intended
bride of her handsome but mad young
cousin. 1968.

Cousin Kate BR 1071
by Georgette Heyer
4 volumes
Kate, an orphaned and penniless
young lady, is befriended by an unknown aunt and installed in luxury at
Staplewood. She begins to suspect
that her aunt's kindness cloaks a cruel
plan and finds that she is the intended
bride of her handsome but mad young
cousin. Published in England. 1968.

The Nonesuch BR 4224
by Georgette Heyer
3 volumes
The most talked-about bachelor in
London society inherits a Yorkshire
estate. The legacy changes his life and
leads him to choose a most unlikely
bride. 1962.

The Reluctant Widow BR 3910
by Georgette Heyer
3 volumes
In Regency England an impoverished
governess applies for a post and arrives at the wrong house. Hurriedly
married to a dying man who has been
stabbed, the rags-to-riches heroine
inherits his estate and endures the
subsequent mysterious events which
occur there. 1946.

The Stanbroke Girls BR 4772
by Fiona Hill
2 volumes
Romance, wit, and nineteenth-century
high style accompany the Stanbroke
girls—impulsive Lady Isabella and her
young sister, Lady Elizabeth. Elizabeth is mad for a detestable rake,
while Isabella seems a perfect match
for a very eligible bachelor who is as
unattainable as he is desirable. 1981.

Rebel Heiress   BR 4080
by Jane Aiken Hodge
2 volumes
On the eve of the War of 1812, Henrietta Marchmont, a bold Yankee woman from Boston, sails to London to claim her rightful place in her father's family, the powerful Marchmont dynasty. She encounters unexpected complications of head and heart. 1975.

The Day of the Butterfly   BR 4241
by Norah Lofts
3 volumes
When Daisy Holt is fired from her first job as a nursemaid, her luck goes from bad to worse, and she seems destined for a life in a London brothel. But her radiance attracts the eye of an artist, and Daisy experiences her first romance and the first of her sorrows as well. 1979.

Gothic Romances

Discs

Strathgallant   RD 17544
by Laura Black
narrated by Rachel Gurney
4 discs
Indomitable Countess Selina announces that her ward, seventeen-
year-old Perdita, will inherit the estate
of Strathgallant if she marries one of
her four cousins. Unwittingly, Selina
sets in motion some nefarious
schemes, for the prize of Strathgallant
proves such a lure that two of the
competitors are murdered. 1981.

Lady of Monkton   RD 13198
by Elizabeth Byrd
narrated by Michael McCullough
3 discs
Married by proxy to a man she has
never met, fourteen-year-old Cathryn
Grandison finds herself ensnarled in a
web of romance, intrigue, and witch-
craft in fifteenth-century Scotland.
Some explicit descriptions of sex.
1975.

The Witch from the Sea   RD 8218
by Philippa Carr
narrated by Dale Carter
4 discs
A tempestuous woman jilts her unex-
citing fiance to marry an arrogant ad-
venturer. Arriving at the forbidding
Castle Paling, she finds strange events
taking place. 1975.

Limmerston Hall   RD 6576
by Hester W. Chapman
narrated by Mitzi Friedlander
3 discs
A woman who looks after her sister's
orphaned children is suspicious of
their brooding artist guardian and
fears his irrational behavior. 1972.

The House at Sandalwood   RD 13880
by Virginia Coffman
narrated by Peggy Schoditsch
4 discs
Unjustly convicted of the murder of
her sister-in-law, Judith Cameron
spent nine years in prison. Now on
parole, she is summoned to a lush
Hawaiian island to care for a childish
niece. She soon becomes enmeshed in
a web of love, murder, intrigue, and
ancient superstition. 1974.

Ravenscroft   RD 9437
by Dorothy Eden
narrated by Pat Gilbert-Read
4 discs
Two orphaned sisters in Victorian
England find themselves trapped by
procurers in London. A nobleman interested in social reform rescues the
girls. 1965.

Hammersleigh   RD 10468
by Rosemary Ellerbeck
narrated by Etain O'Malley
3 discs
Recently widowed Karen Blackwood
returns to her childhood home in
Scotland and encounters Hugh Fuller-
ton, now master of the great manor

house. When she begins a new career as a painter, she finds she is the victim of psychic forces. 1976.

Darsham's Tower   RD 6793
by Harriet Esmond
narrated by Dale Carter
3 discs
A sea captain's daughter is called to Darsham Tower in the English village of Senwich to supervise the young daughter of aristocratic Oliver Darsham. She soon finds herself involved with Oliver as well. 1973.

A Touch of Terror   RD 13939
by Sarah Farrant
narrated by Meg Wynn-Owen
4 discs
In England in 1860, young Laura Lamborne, unable to support herself, agrees through the advice of her aunt to marry mysteriously invalided Sir Matthew Merrick, whom she never sees. Although he is isolated in his curtained bed and surrounded by menacing servants, she falls in love with his beautiful voice as he relates exotic stories of adventure to her. 1979.

A Bride for Bedivere   RD 11864
by Hilary Ford
narrated by Barbara Warner
3 discs
A spirited young woman, the oldest in a family of five fatherless and destitute children, agrees to live on Sir Donald Bedivere's Cornwall estate in exchange for support of her family.

When she learns about the chilling plans for her future, her resolution wavers. 1976.

Seaview Manor   RD 9720
by Elissa Grandower
narrated by Mitzi Friedlander
4 discs
Romance and suspense await Andrea Leighton at Seaview Manor, off the coast of Connecticut. When she discovers three murders, she realizes that at any moment she could be the fourth victim. 1976.

Kilgaren   RD 7315
by Isabelle Holland
narrated by Dale Carter
3 discs
Upon receipt of a letter from her half-brother Jonathan, eighteen-year-old Barbara embarks reluctantly on a journey to her ancestral home in the West Indies. There she finds deception, danger, and unexpected romance. 1974.

The Lost Madonna   RD 17501
by Isabelle Holland
narrated by Mitzi Friedlander
4 discs
In an ancient castle in Italy, young Julia Winthrop is caught up in a web of intrigue, psychic visions, and romance when she learns that her step-grandmother has been murdered and a priceless work of art is missing from the family chapel. 1981.

Moncrieff   RD 9388
by Isabelle Holland
narrated by Dale Carter
4 discs
Editor Antonia Moncrieff inherits a valuable, but eerie, rundown house in Brooklyn Heights. Mysterious circumstances involve her precocious twelve-year-old son, her half-mad former husband, and her old lover, who was blinded in an automobile accident. 1975.

The House of a Thousand Lanterns RD 7371
by Victoria Holt
narrated by Virginia Cromer
2 discs
A marriage of convenience to an elderly man leads a housekeeper's daughter to Hong Kong and the House of a Thousand Lanterns, where she finds she is unwanted and her life is in danger. 1974.

The King of the Castle   RD 9324
by Victoria Holt
narrated by Terry Hayes Sales
5 discs
In the south of France at the turn of the century, Dallas Lawson is hired to restore the art collection of the aloof but attractive Comte de la Talle, who is rumored to have murdered his wife. Dallas becomes involved in danger as well as romance. 1967.

Lord of the Far Island   RD 8499
by Victoria Holt
narrated by Dale Carter
4 discs
In turn-of-century London and Far Island, Ellen is raised by wealthy cousins as a companion to their daughter. Courted by fun-loving Philip, son of a powerful family, Ellen senses impending doom as a recurrent nightmare haunts her. 1975.

Mistress of Mellyn   RD 11268
by Victoria Holt
narrated by Michael McCullough
2 discs
Martha Leigh, a young English governess, takes charge of the motherless child of the enigmatic master of a sinister mansion in Cornwall. She discovers her pupil's mother was murdered, and that she is in danger of the same fate. 1960.

The Fateful Summer   RD 17243
by Velda Johnston
narrated by Becky Parker
2 discs
A turn-of-the-century tale narrated by Emma, who recalls the tragic love affair of her beautiful friend Amanda and the violence that touched all their lives. When Amanda's tyrannical father is found murdered, her lover is the prime suspect. Emma, however, accidentally unearths the true culprit, thereby putting her own life in danger. 1981.

Loving Sands, Deadly Sands   RD 8167
by Charlotte Keppel
narrated by Roy Avers
3 discs
During 1798 when a French invasion
is feared, a colonel and his daughters
live at a country estate next to a
prison for French POWs. Escaped
prisoners, intrigues, and murder are
the ingredients of this romantic suspense novel. 1974.

Prey of the Eagle   RD 8104
by Phyllis G. Leonard
narrated by Anne Pitoniak
4 discs
Danger and passion envelop a Boston
lady in her Mexican mansion, where
an ancestress was sacrificed in an ancient rite. 1974.

**Return to Wuthering Heights
RD 12039**
by Anna L'Estrange
narrated by Richard Clarke
2 discs
A modern sequel to *Wuthering
Heights*. Catherine's daughter, young
Cathy, is happy as the wife of Earnshaw Hareton. History repeats itself,
however, with the appearance of
Heathcliff's natural son, who woos
Cathy away to Wuthering Heights.
1977.

The Flight of the Shadow   RD 20264
by George MacDonald
narrated by Patricia Kilgarriff
3 discs
Against a backdrop of the untamed
Scottish highlands, an orphan raised
by a kindly but brooding uncle falls in
love with her handsome neighbor. His
mother, Lady Lucretia Cairnedge, op-
poses the marriage with such vicious
manipulation that she decides the fate
of two noble families and unearths a
guilty secret that was buried many
years before. 1983.

Sarton Kell   RD 11253
by Kate Mallory
narrated by Mitzi Friedlander
4 discs
At the end of the nineteenth century,
Olivia leaves the South to study art in
New York. There she meets and marries Chris Sarton, half-breed son of an
upstate New York pioneer and his
second wife, Mohawk Annie-Lo. The
newlyweds live at Sarton Kell, a
brooding marble mansion, which
Olivia believes is haunted. 1977.

The Jeweled Daughter   RD 9438
by Anne Maybury
narrated by Elizabeth Swain
3 discs
In Hong Kong, investigating a new
acquisition for a ruthless viscountess,
jewel specialist Sarah Brent meets
with danger and her estranged husband. 1976.

25

The Minerva Stone   RD 11861
by Anne Maybury
narrated by Michael McCullough
2 discs
Set in an old English castle on a cliff above the sea, this story involves Sarah Rhodes, whose marriage appears to be failing; her self-centered husband, who is a television personality; and a former lover. 1968.

The Moonlit Door   RD 11570
by Anne Maybury
narrated by Terry Hayes Sales
3 discs
Though Rachel has dreamed of being mistress of the elegant French castle on the hill, the stately home becomes an eerie setting for vengeance, murder, and bittersweet romance. 1977.

The Pavilion at Monkshood   RD 13073
by Anne Maybury
narrated by Terry Hayes Sales
3 discs
A vulnerable young woman suspects that her lover is dallying nightly with her cousin in an isolated pavilion on the estate. Her heartache grows when she realizes that he is also part of the grim secret of Monkshood. 1965.

Wings of the Falcon   RD 11856
by Barbara Michaels
narrated by Dale Carter
4 discs
After the death of her English artist father, Francesca travels to Italy to join the aristocratic Italian family of her long-dead mother. There she meets her eccentric grandfather; unravels the identity of the Falcon, the mysterious local revolutionary; and finds romance. 1977.

Image of a Lover   RD 8142
by Elisabeth Ogilvie
narrated by Suzanne Toren
5 discs
Seafair Belle, a young music teacher invited by her pupil Miranda to visit the family's summer place off Maine, falls hopelessly in love with Miranda's cousin Patrick. A psychopath loose on the island brings chaos and murder to her stay. 1974.

The Doom of Glendour   RD 13659
by Kate Ostrander
narrated by Catherine Byers
4 discs
A young woman accepts an invitation to become social secretary for her Aunt Jane in Glendour Castle in the Scottish highlands. She becomes an unwilling pawn in an ancient feud between her relations and the Rosswyn clan, her romance with Duncan Rosswyn is opposed, and her life is endangered. 1975.

Devil-May-Care   RD 11615
by Elizabeth Peters
narrated by Eugenia Rawls
3 discs
When Ellie agrees to house sit at her eccentric aunt's mansion in Virginia, she finds herself on the receiving end of a number of ghostly visitations. She also finds romance. 1977.

Dragonmede RD 7292
by Rona Randall
narrated by Mitzi Friedlander
4 discs
When beautiful young Eustacia arrives at Dragonmede as the bride of an eligible nobleman, she discovers he has an uncontrolled passion for gambling. 1974.

Watchman's Stone RD 9084
by Rona Randall
narrated by Dale Carter
3 discs
Despite a disturbing premonition, heiress Elizabeth marries Calum, the Laird of Faillie. She finds herself plagued by an arrogant housekeeper, a surly gardener, and an aura of evil surrounding the isolated Scottish fortress of which she is mistress. 1975.

Dark Inheritance RD 9314
by Carola Salisbury
narrated by Yolande Baven
4 discs
After the death of her tavern-keeper husband, Susannah becomes a governess for the arrogant Devaines of Cornwall. She falls in love with Mark, their son and heir, who mysteriously sends her off to Venice. 1975.

Dragonwyck RD 9962
by Anya Seton
narrated by Janis Gray
6 discs
In the early 1900s at the sinister Hudson River estate of dashing Nicholas Van Ryn, Miranda Wells, a distant cousin and innocent young farm girl, arrives as governess to Nicholas's small daughter. Eventually Miranda becomes the second Mrs. Van Ryn, but finds danger rather than happiness. 1944.

A Wreath of Orchids   RD 14048
by Marjorie Shoebridge
narrated by Rachel Gurney
3 discs
When Venetia Duluth, a shy young bride of a few weeks, is widowed, she journeys to her husband's estate, Garfield Priory, to meet his relatives. Her brief stay is laced with "accidents" that almost drive her to marry again for protection. 1978.

Guinever's Gift RD 11240
by Nicole St. John
narrated by Barbara Caruso
3 discs
Lydian Wentworth marries Lord Charles Ransome, an Arthurian scholar twice her age. While they are excavating for King Arthur's tomb, she encounters hostility from Charles's beautiful cousin and becomes increasingly attracted to his young assistant. 1977.

Turkish Rondo RD 17903
by Anne Stevenson
narrated by Hillary Ryan Norton
3 discs
On a steamer bound for Istanbul, a young Englishwoman helps a stranger escape two murderous attackers. She falls in love and, soon after, impetu-

Gothic Romances Discs, Cassettes

ously marries him. Then he disappears on a mysterious mission, and the intrepid heroine chases clues and her husband through the wilds of Greece and Turkey. 1981.

Touch Not the Cat   RD 10188
by Mary Stewart
narrated by Adale O'Brien
4 discs
Tale about a phantom lover, an ancestral home, a father's strange dying words, and a spirited young Englishwoman with the "gift," who discovers that her lover may be her father's killer. Bestseller. 1976.

The Wild Hunt   RD 10098
by Jill Tattersall
narrated by Elizabeth Swain
3 discs
A kind godfather, a beautiful and brave heroine, a handsome lord, secret rooms, and masked riders figure prominently in this novel. Chantal, hired in 1818 as a governess in a gloomy English house, finds herself subjected to terrifying experiences. 1975.

Abbey Court   RD 10242
by Marcella Thum
narrated by Mitzi Friedlander
4 discs
After her mother's death, Meg leaves Boston for Abbey Court, Ireland, to search for the truth to her past. Exploring her new surroundings, she finds some answers, some romance, and much suspense. 1976.

Hunter's Green   RD 8301
by Phyllis A. Whitney
narrated by Terry Hayes Sales
4 discs
A novel centering around a cryptic message about a chess game. Determined to win back her husband's love, Eve returns to his English estate, where a sinister force seems to mark her for death. 1968.

Thunder Heights   RD 13083
by Phyllis A. Whitney
narrated by Dale Carter
3 discs
When orphaned Camilla King visits her dying grandfather, who founded Thunder Heights on the banks of the Hudson River, she does not know she is about to become the mistress of his huge estate. Along with this fortune, she also inherits a legacy of hate and violence. 1960.

Cassettes

Ravenburn   RC 13642
by Laura Black
narrated by Diane Eilenberg
3 cassettes
In nineteenth-century Scotland eighteen-year-old Katie Irvine is treated like a stepchild since the death of her father, Lord Ravenburn. She has few clothes, little society, and only the outdoors and books as companions. Drawn to a little local island, Katie finds a true friend and love in the isle's abandoned ruined castle. Also

28

issued on flexible disc as FD 13642. 1978.

North Sea Mistress: Romance and Revolution in Modern-Day Scotland RC 11771
by Katrinka Blickle
narrated by Azaleigh Maginnis
2 cassettes
Fiona Grimsby, daughter of a New England college professor, meets her charming millionaire husband-to-be in Scotland. Shortly after their marriage, he dies in an accident and Fiona marries another charmer—only to find her life in danger. 1977.

Shadows on the Tor RC 12203
by Susan Brand
narrated by Barbara Caruso
2 cassettes
A young American sculptress comes to a picturesque Scottish village to recover from a disastrous love affair. She meets fellow artist Jamie Drummond, a stormy-tempered young Scot, who is rumored to have caused the death of his wife. 1977.

The Long Masquerade RC 18481
by Madeleine Brent
narrated by Becky Parker
3 cassettes
A nineteenth-century romance takes its heroine from the aristocracy of colonial Jamaica to the gambling world of London. Young Emma Delaney marries the wealthiest man in Jamaica and learns on their honeymoon that her husband is depraved. Fleeing the island after his bizarre death, she escapes with a former servant in a small boat and begins a long, fearful masquerade. 1981.

Saraband for Two Sisters RC 12834
by Philippa Carr
narrated by Dale Carter
3 cassettes
Set in seventeenth-century England, a time and place of political dissension when Cavalier and Puritan were engaged in power struggles, the story is told by the seventeen-year-old twin daughters of a Cavalier family. Angelet is gentle and romantic, while Bersaba is sensual and an egotistical realist. Complications arise when they both fall in love with Cavalier Richard Tolworthy. Followed by *Song of the Siren (RC 19882)*. 1976.

Song of the Siren RC 19882
by Philippa Carr
narrated by Dale Carter
2 cassettes
During the Jacobite rebellion in England, the passionate Carlotta Endersby flees to France with her fugitive lover, but not before abandoning her husband and satisfying her lusty whims with the would-be suitor of her half sister. Sequel to *Saraband for Two Sisters (RC 12834)*. 1980

The Curse of the Clan RC 10836
by Barbara Cartland
narrated by Yvonne Fair Tessler
1 cassette
Seventeen-year-old Tara finds herself

terrified and dazed—for she has just married a duke she had never seen until two minutes before the wedding. Also issued on flexible disc as FD 10836. 1977.

A Cry in the Night RC 19772
by Mary Higgins Clark
narrated by Bets Thompson
2 cassettes
Jenny MacPartland, the struggling divorced mother of two small girls, meets and marries handsome, wealthy artist Erich Krueger, who takes her and her children away to his family mansion in Minnesota. Erich becomes brooding and rageful and Jenny discovers that he is obsessed with the memory of his dead mother, Caroline. 1982.

Lady of Mallow RC 11528
by Dorothy Eden
narrated by Barbara Bookhammer
2 cassettes
The inheritance of a magnificent country estate, Mallow Hall, is contested. Sarah Mildmay, fiancée of the rightful owner, defies danger and masquerades as a governess in the home of the pretender. 1960.

The Shadow Wife RC 12665
by Dorothy Eden
narrated by Yolande Baven
2 cassettes
Luise Amberley, an impulsive English girl traveling in Majorca, meets and, after a whirlwind courtship, marries Otto Winther, a charming Danish widower. Otto, an epileptic, waits until Luise is pregnant before taking her home to his ancestral castle, where she is greeted with inexplicable animosity. 1967.

The Storrington Papers RC 12822
by Dorothy Eden
narrated by Elizabeth Swain
2 cassettes
Sarah, a young English divorcée, is hired by paralyzed Major Charles Storrington to live in his great Victorian house and ghost-write the family history. With Charles's wife away most of the time, Sarah finds herself falling in love with him and fascinated by the diary of a former Victorian governess who lived there. 1978.

The House of Kuragin RC 11048
by Constance Heaven
narrated by Dale Carter
2 cassettes
In 1820 near St. Petersburg, a genteel, impoverished Englishwoman accepts a position as teacher to the sickly but lovable child of a wealthy count and falls in love with the count's younger brother. 1972.

Wildcliffe Bird RC 19671
by Constance Heaven
narrated by Madelyn Buzzard
3 cassettes
Juliet Prior leaves Paris for her native England when a runaway carriage "accidentally" kills her father. She becomes a servant to her jealous Aunt Harriet but soon accepts a position at

the Chartley mansion in the north country, where she hopes to meet Lady Chartley's nephew Richard. Juliet discovers a web of mysterious accidents and murder among the Chartley clan. 1983.

Watch the Wall   RC 12345
by Jane Aiken Hodge
narrated by Mitzi Friedlander
2 cassettes
When a young American girl visits her English grandfather, she discovers that her cousin Ross is a smuggler and secret agent in danger from both Napoleon and the British. She becomes engaged to Ross to please her grandfather and is soon up to her ears in intrigue and danger. 1966.

Tower Abbey   RC 14485
by Isabelle Holland
narrated by Janet Marchmont
3 cassettes
At the urgent request of an old acquaintance, New York editor Candida Brown, with her many pets, reluctantly goes to Tower Abbey, a vast mansion overlooking the Hudson River. There she falls in love and attempts to break the spell of doom that haunts the place. 1978.

Bride of Pendorric   RC 10476
by Victoria Holt
narrated by Pat Gilbert-Read
2 cassettes
A young woman marries the master of a castle on the coast of Cornwall, scarcely knowing him. The suspense builds when she learns of the legend that the previous bride of Pendorric cannot rest in her grave until a second bride has met her death. 1963.

The Judas Kiss   RC 18787
by Victoria Holt
narrated by Charlotte Stanton
2 cassettes
Pippa Ewing learns that her beloved older sister Francine has been murdered with her husband, Baron Rudolph. In attempting to solve her sister's murder, she journeys to the Duchy of Bruxenstein and takes a job as a governess. There she has a romantic encounter with handsome Conrad and unravels the mystery. 1981.

Menfreya in the Morning   RC 19054
by Victoria Holt
narrated by Laura Giannarelli
2 cassettes
At the turn of the century, a poor little rich girl with one leg shorter than the other, marries and moves to Menfreya, a fortress-like mansion on the Cornish coast, where mystery ensues. 1966.

On the Night of the Seventh Moon
RC 15985
by Victoria Holt
narrated by Mitzi Friedlander
3 cassettes
According to an ancient Black Forest legend, the god of mischief prevails on the Night of the Seventh Moon.

An English girl visiting Germany, the land of her mother's birth, discovers intrigue, adventure, and romance lurking on this special day. 1972.

The Pride of the Peacock   RC 11693
by Victoria Holt
narrated by Dale Carter
2 cassettes
Jessica Clavering's unique inheritance compels her to marry an opal mining executive, whom she dislikes. In Australia she encounters the mystery and evil surrounding a rare opal and discovers her growing love for her husband. 1976.

The Dark Shore   RC 11091
by Susan Howatch
narrated by Michael Clarke-Laurence
2 cassettes
A young woman gradually discovers the truth about her husband and his family at his estate on the Cornish moors. 1965.

The Waiting Sands   RC 16464
by Susan Howatch
narrated by Don Emmick
1 cassette
Rachel Lord senses impending disaster at a birthday celebration at Roshven. The setting is perfect for the dark, handsome Daniel Carey, who both attracts and frightens her. 1966.

Tarot's Tower   RC 12053
by Jennie Melville
narrated by Michael McCullough
2 cassettes
Christable Warwick takes over her family's restored observatory in the English countryside, ostensibly to watch a comet but actually to keep a rendezvous with her childhood sweetheart Piers. Piers turns out to have been killed in a hit-and-run accident the year before, and many suspect it was murder. Then Chris begins to get letters from her dead love. 1978.

Pencarnan   RC 12346
by Jennifer Rigg
narrated by Michael McCullough
2 cassettes
When an heiress's sweetheart returns from World War I with amnesia and no memory of their past love, she agrees to marry him anyway. They go to Pencarnan, his ancestral home in Wales. There she becomes the victim of a terrible fate that nearly destroys her. 1977.

The Winter Bride   RC 12850
by Carola Salisbury
narrated by Michael McCullough
2 cassettes
A young woman's admiration for a distinguished poet leads her to accept a position as his secretary at the eerie castle Malmaynes. Despite a sense of foreboding, a tender romance blossoms between them. 1978.

The Trembling Hills   RC 17045
by Phyllis A. Whitney
narrated by Peg Munson
3 cassettes
When a young woman comes to live in a San Francisco mansion in 1908, she is caught up in the romance and intrigue of the old house. 1956.

Window on the Square   RC 12376
by Phyllis A. Whitney
narrated by Mitzi Friedlander
2 cassettes
When Meegan Kincaid is hired as companion to moody nine-year-old Jeremy, she discovers that Jeremy is supposed to have shot his father and that his mother has married the dead husband's brother. 1962.

The Haversham Legacy   RC 8051
by Daoma Winston
narrated by Eugenia Rawls
6 cassettes
In post-Civil War Washington, D.C., Miranda first experiences the curse of the Haversham Square mansion when a relative commits murder because of his love for her. Even after Miranda marries her true love, her happiness is marred by a series of tragedies. 1974.

The Medea Legend   RC 10089
by Elizabeth York
narrated by Dale Carter
2 cassettes
When seventeen-year-old Anne is summoned to Margrave House by her mysterious guardian, her aunt tells her to trust no one. Only love saves her from family tragedy and a psychic battle waged from beyond the grave. 1975.

Braille

The Smile of the Stranger   BR 4177
by Joan Aiken
4 volumes
Juliana Paget and her dying father, an expatriate writer living in Italy, are forced to return to the ancestral mansion in Regency England. Once there Juliana must contend with troublesome relatives, worthless suitors, and murderous assaults until she finds her true love. 1978.

Ravenburn   BR 4046
by Laura Black
5 volumes
In nineteenth-century Scotland, eighteen-year-old Katie Irvine is treated like a stepchild since the death of her father, Lord Ravenburn. She has few clothes, little society, and only the outdoors and books as companions. Drawn to a little local island, Katie finds a true friend and love in the isle's abandoned ruined castle. 1978.

The Capricorn Stone   BR 4365
by Madeleine Brent
3 volumes
Bridie Chance and her sister are reared in luxury in the country home of their delightful father Roger, who is frequently away on business on the Continent. After Roger's accidental

death, he is revealed as a gifted and famous jewel thief. 1979.

Return Match   BR 4152
by Elizabeth Cadell
2 volumes
Back from Brazil to work in London, international playboy Nigel Pressley finds that Rona, his mother's god-daughter, is an ugly duckling turned swan. Rona, however, seems deter-mined to spurn Nigel's overtures until some visitors stir up an old tragedy with sinister aspects. 1979.

The Witch from the Sea   BR 2866
by Philippa Carr
4 volumes
A tempestuous woman jilts her unex-citing fiancé to marry an arrogant ad-venturer. Arriving at the forbidding Castle Paling, she finds strange events taking place. 1975.

A Cry in the Night   BR 5226
by Mary Higgins Clark
3 volumes
Jenny MacPartland, the struggling divorced mother of two small girls, meets and marries handsome, wealthy artist Erich Krueger, who takes her and her children away to his family mansion in Minnesota. Erich becomes brooding and rageful and Jenny dis-covers that he is obsessed with the memory of his dead mother, Caroline. 1982.

The Night of the Party   BR 1837
by Laura Conway
2 volumes
Juliet Alban, living with her aunt in the English countryside, finds herself attracted to a new neighbor and is mysteriously visited by the apparition of her deceased uncle. 1971.

An Important Family   BR 5137
by Dorothy Eden
3 volumes
Romantic young Kate leaves Ireland after her fiancé's death and signs on as a companion to the Devenish fam-ily, who are going to New Zealand. After their arrival, Kate perceives a dark mystery clouding the lives of the family and seeks to find the secret that has driven them so far from home. 1982.

The Property of a Gentleman   BR 2694
by Catherine Gaskin
4 volumes
A young woman antique dealer, called upon to appraise the treasures of the once magnificent Thirlbeck country estate, becomes directly in-volved with the mystery of the old mansion. A blend of romance and his-tory plus an inside look at the deal-ings of a London auction house. 1974.

The Freebody Heiress   BR 2891
by Ethel Edison Gordon
2 volumes
A sensitive, terrified young heiress is convinced that she is a jinx to every-one who comes close to her. A pro-

fessor at Freebody College, whose wife died in a mysterious fire, helps her overcome her fears. 1974.

The House of Kuragin   BR 1864
by Constance Heaven
2 volumes
In 1820 near St. Petersburg, a genteel, impoverished Englishwoman accepts a position as teacher to the sickly but lovable child of a wealthy count and falls in love with the count's younger brother. 1972.

The King of the Castle   BR 556
by Victoria Holt
4 volumes
In the south of France at the turn of the century, Dallas Lawson is hired to restore the art collection of the aloof but attractive Comte de la Talle, who is rumored to have murdered his wife. Dallas finds herself involved in danger as well as romance. 1967.

Lord of the Far Island   BR 3047
by Victoria Holt
3 volumes
In turn-of-century London and Far Island, Ellen is raised by wealthy cousins as a companion to their daughter. Courted by fun-loving Philip, son of a powerful family, Ellen senses impending doom as a recurrent nightmare haunts her. 1975.

The Mask of the Enchantress   BR 4615
by Victoria Holt
3 volumes
Joel Mateland and his lover Anabel

take their illegitimate child Suewellyn from England to primitive Vulcan Island in the South Pacific after Joel kills his evil brother and flees his ancestral home, Mateland Castle. After many peaceful years, Suewellyn, now a young woman, is alarmed when her double, Joel's legitimate daughter, shows up to make mischief. 1980.

The Pride of the Peacock   BR 3348
by Victoria Holt
3 volumes
Jessica Clavering's unique inheritance compels her to marry an opal mining executive whom she dislikes. In Australia she encounters the mystery and evil surrounding a rare opal and discovers her growing love for her husband. 1976.

The Waiting Sands   BR 2422
by Susan Howatch
2 volumes
Rachel Lord senses impending disaster at a birthday celebration at Roshven. The setting is perfect for dark, handsome Daniel Carey, who both attracts and frightens her. 1966.

The Fateful Summer   BR 5001
by Velda Johnston
2 volumes
A turn-of-the-century tale narrated by Emma, who recalls the tragic love affair of her beautiful friend Amanda and the violence that touched all their lives. When Amanda's tyrannical father is found murdered, her lover is the prime suspect. Emma, however,

accidentally unearths the true culprit, thereby putting her own life in danger. 1981.

Other Karen   BR 5648
by Velda Johnston
2 volumes
An aspiring young actress in Manhattan, Catherine Mayhew, responds to an ad in the *Village Voice* offering a part in a regional theater production. The role turns out to be a real-life deception for an old woman, whose dying days will be more pleasant if she believes her long-lost granddaughter has come home at last. But Catherine herself is deceived as she discovers a murderous plot and risks her own life. 1983.

A Presence in an Empty Room BR 4637
by Velda Johnston
2 volumes
When Susan Hapgood marries widower Martin Summerslee after a whirlwind courtship, it looks as if she will live happily ever after. He takes her to live in the lovely old family mansion in Maine, but Susan finds an oppressive "presence" there that she soon realizes is both dangerous and threatening. 1980.

Loving Sands, Deadly Sands   BR 2934
by Charlotte Keppel
2 volumes
During 1798 when a French invasion is feared, a colonel and his daughters live at a country estate next to a

prison for French POWs. Escaped prisoners, intrigues, and murder are the ingredients of this romantic suspense novel. 1974.

The Jarrah Tree   BR 3836
by Mary Kistler
2 volumes
In Australia in the 1840s a couple enter a marriage of convenience because he needs a wife to take charge of his orphaned niece and his household, and she wants to be near her fiancé who is a prisoner in Tasmania. Finally she must choose between duty and passion. 1977.

Ride a White Dolphin   BR 3011
by Anne Maybury
2 volumes
When her husband's business takes him to Venice, Leonie lives with her husband's aunt in an old Venetian palace. She knows she is the victim of a series of strange violent accidents, but no one believes her. When she thinks her husband has renewed his love affair with an opera star, she is heartbroken. 1971.

The Cry of the Owl   BR 3832
by Margaret Mayhew
2 volumes
An eighteenth-century tale set on a lonely, eerie English marsh in the great days of smuggling. After the death of her father, Tamazine saves the family home by marrying a notorious distant cousin. 1977.

Black Rainbow   BR 5350
by Barbara Michaels
3 volumes
An ambitious young woman, well-educated but poor, accepts a position as governess at Grayhaven Manor in an ancient Warwickshire village. Ignoring ominous signs, she falls in love with the handsome, brooding owner of the estate and lives to regret it. 1982.

The Sea King's Daughter   BR 4282
by Barbara Michaels
5 volumes
A young American girl is employed by her archaeologist father to dive illegally for Minoan artifacts. As many frightening accidents happen to her on the Greek island of Thera, she at first suspects ancient spirits but finally discovers that a live enemy wants her out of the way. Strong language. 1975.

The Heroine's Sister   BR 3043
by Frances Murray
2 volumes
In mid-nineteenth-century Venice, soon after becoming the governess at the Palazzo Murano, Mary senses that danger threatens the dashing political radical with whom she has fallen in love. 1975.

The Cricket Cage   BR 3323
by R. H. Shimer
3 volumes
A young newspaper woman, summoned by her sister to Seattle in 1886, arrives to find a coffin, suspense, and terror. 1975.

Touch Not the Cat   BR 3302
by Mary Stewart
3 volumes
Tale about a phantom lover, an ancestral home, a father's strange dying words, and a spirited young English-woman with the "gift," who discovers that her lover may be her father's killer. Bestseller. 1976.

Cameron's Landing   BR 3766
by Anne Stuart
2 volumes
In the 1880s on a small island off Maine, Lorna MacDougall takes a position as companion to a formidable old lady, who really wants Lorna to investigate the murder of her husband. Lorna finds herself falling in love with the most likely suspect. 1977.

Lyonesse Abbey   BR 924
by Jill Tattersall
1 volume
To pay a gambling debt, the father of a seventeen-year-old woman gives her in marriage to a mysterious man. He takes her to his family home, a converted monastery high above the sea in Cornwall and a fitting setting for the strange events which follow. 1968.

Gothic Romances

Hunter's Green   BR 2974
by Phyllis A. Whitney
3 volumes
A novel centering around a cryptic message about a chess game. Determined to win back her husband's love, Eve returns to his English estate, where a sinister force seems to mark her for death. 1968.

I, Victoria Strange   BR 3063
by Ruth Willock
2 volumes
A young heiress, afraid that an unknown assassin is following her, abruptly leaves New York for faraway Iceland and Scotland. She finds fleeting happiness with a young Canadian journalist, until strange mishaps make her doubt even his motives. 1975.

Classic Romances

Discs

Northanger Abbey   RD 6737
by Jane Austen
edited by Anne Henry
narrated by Carmen Mathews
3 discs
A satire of nineteenth-century Gothic novels. The daughter of a well-to-do clergyman is taken to Bath for the season by friends. She falls in love with a man but causes difficulties by conjuring up a gruesome mystery about his eccentric father. 1818.

Sanditon   RD 8247
by Jane Austen and another lady
narrated by Carmen Mathews
4 discs
This novel, first begun in 1817, was recently completed by an admirer of the author's. It tells of Charlotte Heywood's stay in the village of Sanditon, a fashionable bathing resort, where she encounters many kinds of people and romance in various guises. 1975.

Rob Roy   RD 14836
by Sir Walter Scott
narrated by Tom Martin
7 discs
In early eighteenth-century England, the son of a rich London merchant refuses to adopt his father's profession and is banished to the home of his fox-hunting, hard-drinking uncle, Sir Hildebrand. He and his cousin become enemies when they both fall in love with the same girl. Rob Roy, a powerful outlaw, comes to his defense. 1818.

The Torrents of Spring   RD 6227
by Ivan Turgenev
translated by David Magarshack
narrated by Alexander Scourby
2 discs
Three stories about the rapture, humiliation, and joy of love, including stories about first love and an unrequited infatuation. 1871.

Cassettes

Mansfield Park   RC 20403
by Jane Austen
edited by Tony Tanner
narrated by Laura Giannarelli
3 cassettes
First published in 1814, this novel tells of Sir Thomas Bertram's family of Mansfield Park, consisting of his selfish and indolent wife, two sons, and two daughters. The Bertrams undertake the charge of nine-year-old Fanny Price, a poor relation. At fifteen, Fanny is dismayed when she sees her cousin Edmund, her only friend, falling in love with the shallow, worldly Mary Crawford, a village newcomer. Eventually Fanny's modesty and honest disposition are rewarded when Edmund wakes up to Mary's frivolous nature. 1966.

Classic Romances Cassettes

Persuasion   RC 10475
by Jane Austen
narrated by Carmen Mathews
2 cassettes
At twenty-seven a woman regrets that she refused to marry the navy captain she loved at nineteen. When her spendthrift father is forced to rent the family estate and move to Bath, she meets her former love again. 1818.

Zuleika Dobson; Or, An Oxford Love Story
RC 18763
by Sir Max Beerbohm
narrated by Patricia Beaudry
2 cassettes
A stunning adventuress descends upon Oxford during Eights Week and captures the heart of every under-graduate student. One of her victims, the Duke of Dorset, is particularly devastated by her beauty. 1911.

Jane Eyre   RC 10886
by Charlotte Bronte
narrated by Rachel Gurney
4 cassettes
Nineteenth-century English novel. An intelligent woman educated at a chari-table institution becomes the govern-ess at an estate, is caught up in the mysteries of the manor, and falls in love with the brooding master of the house. 1847.

Lucy Gayheart   RC 11292
by Willa Cather
narrated by Suzanne Toren
1 cassette
A young girl from a small village goes to Chicago to study music. She falls in love with a middle-aged concert singer, knows a brief moment of deep contentment, and then the pain of separation. 1935.

The Pathfinder; Or, The Inland Sea
RC 11072
by James Fenimore Cooper
narrated by Richard Wulf
4 cassettes
Historical American romance set in 1756 about a fearless wilderness scout in love for the first and only time. 1840.

Tender Is the Night   RC 18133
by F. Scott Fitzgerald
narrated by Alexander Scourby
2 cassettes
An American psychiatrist, studying in Europe in the 1920s, falls in love with a wealthy patient. In their marriage, he reacts against her great depen-dence on him as both husband and doctor before he realizes his equal dependence on her. 1934.

Under the Greenwood Tree; Or, The Mellstock Quire: A Rural Painting of the Dutch School RC 18069
by Thomas Hardy
edited by David Wright
narrated by George Rose
2 cassettes
A nineteenth-century English idyll, set in the rustic village of Mellstock. Tells of two young lovers, Dick Dewy, son of the local carrier, and Fancy Day, the schoolmistress. 1872.

The Well-Beloved: A Sketch of a Temperament   RC 18468
by Thomas Hardy
narrated by Grover Gardner
2 cassettes
Novel set in nineteenth-century London and the Isle of Slinger, where artist Jocelyn Pearston pursues the vision of the ideal woman, whom he recognizes in three generations of one family. 1892.

Across the River and into the Trees RC 7921
by Ernest Hemingway
narrated by Eugene Kressin
3 cassettes
Realizing he will soon die, an American army officer revisits Italy and has an affair with a countess. 1950.

A Farewell to Arms   RC 10857
by Ernest Hemingway
narrated by Gordon Gould
2 cassettes
An American lieutenant serving in the ambulance service in Italy falls in love with an English nurse during World War I. Their love story is told in poetic language and with austere realism to present a powerful argument against war. 1929.

The American   RC 17612
by Henry James
edited by William Spengemann
narrated by Guy Sorel
3 cassettes
A wealthy American in Paris falls in love with a French widow of noble family. Although the match is a good one, the social pressures of the exclusive aristocratic world separate the couple. The cheerful good nature of the American contrasts with the pride and mean-spiritedness of the European nobility. 1876.

The Golden Bowl   RC 14648
by Henry James
narrated by Bradley Bransford
5 cassettes
Maggie Verver, daughter of an American millionaire, lives in London. She marries an indigent Italian prince previously in love with her friend Charlotte, who visits the couple and continues an intimacy with the husband. A valued gift, the fragile and exquisite golden bowl, symbolizes the romantic relationships. 1904.

Lady Chatterley's Lover   RC 14901
by D. H. Lawrence
narrated by Tom Martin
3 cassettes
An earthy love story, once banned in the United States, of the affair between Lady Chatterley and her gamekeeper, Mellors. Married to an impotent, invalid husband, Lady Chatterley is attracted to Mellors' strength and independence from industrial society. Explicit descriptions of sex. 1959.

Women in Love   RC 9569
by D. H. Lawrence
narrated by Hazel Kiley
2 cassettes
The complex love relationships of the two couples explored in this novel reflect the archetypal differences between men and women as the couples battle with themselves and each other to overcome their difficulties. 1920.

Diana of the Crossways   RC 11536
by George Meredith
narrated by Alan Haines
3 cassettes
A witty Irish girl marries a gentleman of limited intelligence. He is unable to appreciate his exceptional wife, who consequently dallies with men who can. 1885.

Gone with the Wind   RC 8025
by Margaret Mitchell
narrated by House Jameson
14 cassettes in three containers
A Civil War epic in which Scarlett O'Hara, a forceful and ruthless heroine, and Rhett Butler, a war profiteer, play out their tempestuous love affair against the background of the war-torn South. Also issued on flexible disc as FD 8025. Pulitzer Prize 1936.

Portrait of Jennie   RC 12361
by Robert Nathan
narrated by Hal Tenny
1 cassette
A girl comes into the life of a poor young artist when he is forlorn and his art is at a standstill. Through her inspiration he becomes famous. 1939.

The Haunted Pool   RC 15946
by George Sand
translated by Frank Hunter Potter
narrated by Suzanne Toren
1 cassette
A peasant widower must choose a new wife to raise his family. 1890.

Mauprat   RC 14285
by George Sand
translated by Stanley Young
narrated by James DeLotel
3 cassettes
Nineteenth-century romantic novel about Bernal de Mauprat, a violent, brutish young man who is driven by love for his cousin, Edmee, to become civilized and well-educated. 1847.

The Bride of Lammermoor   RC 12446
by Sir Walter Scott
narrated by Michael Clarke-Laurence
3 cassettes
The last scion of a ruined family falls in love with the daughter of his ancestral enemy. Prophecies, apparitions, and the opposition of an ambitious mother foreshadow tragic end to the romance. Donizetti's opera "Lucia di Lammermoor" is based on this tale. 1819.

The Charterhouse of Parma   RC 16346
by Maurice Stendhal
translated by C. K. Scott-Moncrieff
narrated by Jonathan Farwell
3 cassettes
Set during the Napoleonic wars, this novel delves into power politics and love. It relates the affair of a brilliant woman who becomes the mistress of a politician to further her adored nephew's career. 1839.

Anna Karenina   RC 12563
by Leo Tolstoy
narrated by Guy Sorel
7 cassettes in two containers
Set in nineteenth-century Russia, this story of the loveless marriage and extramarital love affair of an intense woman deals with the psychology of the characters and the impact of societal morality. 1873-1877.

The Belton Estate   RC 11312
by Anthony Trollope
narrated by Alan Haines
3 cassettes
Clara Amedroz is courted by two men. Both inherited property originally meant for her. Will Belton, her farmer cousin and one of the suitors, eventually wins out over the mean-tempered Captain Aylmer. 1866.

The Claverings   RC 13237
by Anthony Trollope
narrated by Dale Carter
4 cassettes
Story written in mid-nineteenth-century about an English country family at Clavering Park. The youngest son Harry is in love with two women—the beautiful but cruel Julia and the steadfast Florence. 1867.

Dr. Thorne   RC 12410
by Anthony Trollope
narrated by Hal Tenny
4 cassettes
A story about quiet country life in the west of England. Mary Thorne, a sweet, modest girl, lives with her kind uncle in Greshambury, where the young heir of Greshambury Park falls in love with her. 1858.

On the Eve   RC 9102
by Ivan Turgenev
translated by Gilbert Gardiner
narrated by Flo Gibson
3 cassettes
A tragic love story reflecting the shifting society of nineteenth-century Rus-

sia. Before the age of social and political reform, an idealistic young girl with vague yearnings for freedom falls in love with a Bulgarian revolutionary. 1859.

Smoke   RC 9256
by Ivan Turgenev
translated by Natalie Duddington
narrated by Flo Gibson
3 cassettes
The nineteenth-century Russian novelist affirms the strength of love and the tyranny of passion in a tale about the non-political Litvinov and his overwhelming love for the beautiful but treacherous Irina. 1867.

The Web and the Rock   RC 11158
by Thomas Wolfe
narrated by Gordon Gould
6 cassettes
George Webber, a brilliant young writer, goes to the magic city of New York, where he dreams he will find fame, fortune, and the love of beautiful women. A passionate and turbulent love story. Some strong language. 1939.

Marjorie Morningstar   RC 11490
by Herman Wouk
narrated by Mitzi Friedlander
5 cassettes
A pretty Manhattan Jewish girl at age seventeen sets out to become an actress. She falls in love with Noel Airman, a brilliant, enigmatic rake. Some strong language. Also issued on flexible disc as FD 11490. 1955.

Braille

Persuasion   BR 2343
by Jane Austen
3 volumes
At twenty-seven a woman regrets that she refused to marry the navy captain she loved at nineteen. When her spendthrift father is forced to rent the family estate and move to Bath, she meets her former love again. 1818.

Pride and Prejudice   BR 1583
by Jane Austen
4 volumes
An early nineteenth-century English novel of manners centering on five marriageable sisters, particularly the rather nonconformist Elizabeth. 1813.

Sense and Sensibility   BR 2944
by Jane Austen
5 volumes
This novel about two sisters of varying temperaments and how their opposite attitudes affect both their romantic entanglements and their destinies, presents a portrait of upper and middle-class English society of the period. 1811.

Jane Eyre   BR 1216
by Charlotte Bronte
7 volumes
Nineteenth-century English novel. An intelligent woman educated at a charitable institution becomes the governess at an estate, is caught up in the mysteries of the manor, and falls

in love with the brooding master of the house. 1847.

Wuthering Heights   BR 1218
by Emily Bronte
4 volumes
Nineteenth-century English novel, set in the wild moor country of Yorkshire. Heathcliff, a foundling raised in the Earnshaw home, is rough and rugged as the landscape. He passionately loves the daughter Catherine, and dedicates his life to the realization of that love, although society and the Earnshaws are against him. 1847.

Victoria   BR 1728
by Knut Hamsun
translated by Oliver Stallybrass
1 volume
Johannes, a young Norwegian writer and son of a miller, falls deeply in love with the daughter of a landowner, but due to differences in their backgrounds and temperaments they never marry. 1898.

A Farewell to Arms   BR 1599
by Ernest Hemingway
3 volumes
An American lieutenant serving in the ambulance service in Italy falls in love with an English nurse during World War I. Their love story is told in poetic language and with austere realism to present a powerful argument against war. 1929.

Gone with the Wind   BR 1609
by Margaret Mitchell
13 volumes
A Civil War epic in which Scarlett O'Hara, a forceful and ruthless heroine, and Rhett Butler, a war profiteer, play out their tempestuous love affair against the background of the war-torn South. Pulitzer Prize 1936.

Mauprat   BR 4462
by George Sand
translated by Stanley Young
3 volumes
English version of a nineteenth-century romantic novel about Bernal de Mauprat, a violent, brutish young man who is driven by love for his cousin, Edmee, to become civilized and well-educated. 1847.

All's Well that Ends Well   BR 1086
by William Shakespeare
1 volume
A dramatic comedy about a young woman who saves a king's life and is given her choice of husbands. The man she loves does not reciprocate her affection, and the play deals with her clever and devious attempts to claim him legally if not amorously. 1602.

As You Like It   BR 1088
by William Shakespeare
1 volume
A pastoral comedy set primarily in the forest of Arden. A duke is exiled by his cruel brother, who later banishes his daughter as well. The action

switches from the court to the forest, where the exiles and friends frolic, tease, philosophize and discover happiness and true love after wandering in a maze of romances, unrequited loves, and mixed identities. 1600.

Love's Labor's Lost BR 1083
by William Shakespeare
1 volume
A dramatic comedy in which the king of Navarre and his friends swear to avoid the company of women and devote themselves to study for three years. Their plans go awry when the charming princess of France arrives on a diplomatic mission with three vivacious ladies. 1594.

Measure for Measure BR 1085
by William Shakespeare
1 volume
A dramatic comedy about a duke reluctant to enforce chastity laws. He temporarily leaves Vienna in the hands of an overly zealous prosecutor whose past is not entirely blameless. Regarding himself above the law, the prosecutor agrees to free Isabella's brother for a price—Isabella. In order to clear up entanglements and save a life, the duke must reassume leadership. 1604.

A Midsummer Night's Dream BR 1103
by William Shakespeare
1 volume
A seventeenth-century comedy of lovers and fairy revels set in the woods of Athens. With the complexity of three separate plots and mismatched couples, this dramatic farce is complete with spells and enchantments by the king of the fairies and Puck, his mischievous servant. 1594.

Much Ado about Nothing BR 1104
by William Shakespeare
1 volume
A comic drama concerning two pairs of lovers and the complications that arise when a jealous troublemaker slyly casts a shadow on the honor of one of the women. 1598.

Pericles, Prince of Tyre BR 1106
by William Shakespeare
1 volume
The trials of Prince Pericles begin when he suspects the king's incestuous love for his daughter and is banished. He is shipwrecked and marries a foreign princess, who appears to die in childbirth. Years of confusion and mishap precede a joyous family reunion. 1609.

Romeo and Juliet BR 1109
by William Shakespeare
1 volume
A sixteenth-century romantic tragedy of two teenagers from rival families who fall in love. A sentence of exile and an impending arranged marriage force the two to flee. A friar suggests a ruse to accomplish their union, but miscommunication causes it to backfire. 1595.

The Tempest   BR 1111
by William Shakespeare
1 volume
A duke is ousted from his throne and banished with his daughter to an enchanted island. He releases some spellbound spirits, who help him undo his usurper. 1612.

Two Gentlemen of Verona   BR 1116
by William Shakespeare
1 volume
A comedy about two sets of lovers. The infidelity of one of the gentlemen leads to complications and temporary heartbreak, but the constancy of one woman brings her success in love. 1595.

More Romances

Discs

Enchanted Oasis   RD 14004
by Faith Baldwin
narrated by Michael McCullough
3 discs
A young, wealthy, shy English girl is suddenly introduced into the sophisticated society of a Palm Springs resort and falls in love with a young rancher. She encounters serious difficulties before winning him. 1966.

The Lonely Man   RD 17256
by Faith Baldwin
narrated by Jim Walton
3 discs
A young doctor with a busy practice in a small New England town mourns the death of his wife. But even a busy man gets lonely—and Frances Lawson, a beautiful, rich divorcee has designs on him. 1964.

New Girl in Town   RD 9548
by Faith Baldwin
narrated by Janis Gray
2 discs
Maggie arrives from Hawaii determined to make a new life for herself in the wonderful house in New England that Aunt Hattie bequeathed to her. One of her first new friends is lawyer Matt Comstock, the most eligible bachelor in town. 1975.

No Bed of Roses   RD 7024
by Faith Baldwin
narrated by Mitzi Friedlander
2 discs
The marriage of a woman who is a real estate agent and a man who is the owner of a bookstore is tested when another woman enters the scene with the discovery of a manuscript. 1973.

Thursday's Child   RD 10215
by Faith Baldwin
narrated by Shirley Reynolds
3 discs
Set in a gracious small village in New England where Sara Foster comes to live with her aristocratic grandmother. Sara takes a job at a friend's bookshop, meets co-owner Sam Peters and Paul Stevens, a playboy, and finally decides to marry one of them. 1976.

Time and the Hour   RD 7567
by Faith Baldwin
narrated by Dale Carter
3 discs
Recently divorced, a young artist rents a studio in little Oxford, where she becomes involved in the life of the townspeople and with a handsome architect. 1974.

Regatta Summer   RD 8475
by Elizabeth Deare Bennett
narrated by Tom Martin
2 discs
The elegant lives and scandalous loves of an aristocratic Edwardian family. Until she meets the self-assured

American Langdon Hill, Lady Alix Tinsdel always has the upper hand with her lovers. Strong language and some explicit descriptions of sex. 1974.

The Borgia Prince   RD 9722
by Pamela Bennetts
narrated by George Patterson
4 discs
Cesare Borgia pledges to subdue the beautiful woman he has captured at the castle of San Savarno. When she finally succumbs to him, they discover their love for one another. 1968.

People in Glass Houses   RD 8345
by Charity Blackstock
narrated by Terry Hayes Sales
4 discs
In a small apartment house in London, a gentle romance blossoms between Rose, a sympathetic woman in her thirties with two young children, and a Czech refugee doctor who lives on the floor above her. Rose, separated from her homosexual husband, finds the courage to divorce him. Strong language. 1975.

Embrace and Conquer   RD 18270
by Jennifer Blake
narrated by Catherine Byers
4 discs
Felicite, the daughter of a wealthy New Orleans merchant, is forced to become the mistress of the mysterious Captain Morgan McCormack in order to help free her father from prison. When she learns of her father's death,

she attempts to flee to France, but she is captured by pirates and is closely pursued by McCormack. Some descriptions of sex. 1981.

The Flame of the Borgias   RD 8492
by Jean Briggs
narrated by Hal Tenny
5 discs
A historical tale that portrays the fiery love affair between Lucrezia Borgia and a Venetian nobleman and future cardinal. The account is inspired by the early sixteenth-century correspondence between the lovers. Some strong language. 1974.

The Sandalwood Fan   RD 19830
by Diana Brown
narrated by Becky Parker
3 discs
In eighteenth-century England, a young widow once cruelly abused by a much older husband is now forced to live under the tyranny of his executor. She shuns self-pity and uses her artistic talent to capture the beauty of nature on canvas. It is this sensitivity and spirit that finally wins the heart of Lord Charles. 1983.

The Last Romantic   RD 14040
by Dorothea Buske
narrated by Barbara Caruso
3 discs
Martha first meets Celia, an educated-in-France orphan, in 1927 at the posh Severn School, and becomes obsessively devoted to the lovely, self-possessed Celia. Later Celia captures the

heart of Martha's childhood soulmate Austin, though self-sacrificing Martha still cares for him. When Celia leaves Austin for a career in art, Martha hopes to regain her true love. 1979.

The Corner Shop   RD 9378
by Elizabeth Cadell
narrated by Suzanne Toren
2 discs
A director of a secretarial agency decides to inquire into the dismissal of three of her most efficient secretaries by the absentminded Professor Hallam. 1966.

Game in Diamonds   RD 9554
by Elizabeth Cadell
narrated by Norman Barrs
3 discs
The grandson of Lady Charlotte Merrion, though engaged to another woman, begins a delicate romance with a student visiting his grandmother's mansion. While wandering about the estate, the couple happens upon a mystery surrounding an ancient brick tower. 1976.

The Haymaker   RD 14939
by Elizabeth Cadell
narrated by Dale Carter
3 discs
Neither Stapling Manor nor any of the fine family possessions of this stately home really belongs to Lady Laura, but for more than twenty years she has enjoyed them undisturbed. No one is worried except old Cosmo Brierley, trustee of the estate, who

has no control over the eccentric aristocrat. But when the owner of the estate arrives from America, there are surprises in store. 1972.

Royal Summons   RD 6496
by Elizabeth Cadell
narrated by Janis Gray
3 discs
A plain woman arrives from Arizona to inspect the estate she has inherited from her mother's English family, and there meets a young archaeologist. 1973.

The Toy Sword   RD 10200
by Elizabeth Cadell
narrated by Burt Blackwell
3 discs
Debonair Edmund Forth rescues young Fran Nash while vacationing in Portugal. Not as helpless as she appears, Fran complicates his life. 1962.

The Adulteress   RD 19845
by Philippa Carr
narrated by Michael McCullough
5 discs
When in mid-eighteenth-century England, Zipporah Ransome sets out for her family's ancestral home, she is a sensible, happily married young woman. But the visit changes her, and she leaves pregnant with the child of a handsome stranger who will dominate her life and fortune more powerfully than she could ever have imagined. Second part of a series. Followed by *Knave of Hearts (RD 20261)*. 1982.

Knave of Hearts   RD 20261
by Philippa Carr
narrated by Michael McCullough
4 discs
Lottie arrives at her father's house in France, a girl with a woman's beauty and desires. At first lonely for her beloved English countryside and the boy she has always adored, she is soon swept away by the glitter of Louis XV's Paris. Third part of a series. Sequel to *The Adulteress (RD 19845)*. 1983.

The Lion Triumphant   RD 7242
by Philippa Carr
narrated by Terry Hayes Sales
5 discs
During the reign of Elizabeth I, the dashing sea captain Jake Pennlyon sails into the life of headstrong Catherine. Theirs is a tempestuous, though seemingly cursed, romance. 1974.

The Love Child   RD 13158
by Philippa Carr
narrated by Meg Wynn-Owen
4 discs
Set against the post-Reformation background of England. Priscilla Eversleigh, at fourteen, has an impassioned love affair with a man on the run from religious and political troubles. He is captured by the king's men and beheaded before Priscilla secretly bears his child. Second part of a series. Sequel to *The Miracle at St. Bruno's (RD 6121)*. 1978.

The Miracle at St. Bruno's   RD 6121
by Philippa Carr
narrated by Mitzi Friedlander
5 discs
Set during the sinister and uncertain times of Henry VIII's England, the tale is told by a young woman, daughter of a beheaded lawyer, who marries an appealing man of questionable birth. Tragedy looms as both the young man and a treasure vanish. First part of a series. Followed by *The Love Child (RD 13158)*. 1972.

**Will You Love Me in September
RD 17919**
by Philippa Carr
narrated by Michael McCullough
5 discs
Though Clarissa is only twelve when she first encounters Lance Clavering, she is not too young to fall in love, nor to become the pawn in a deadly game of power and passion. The time is 1715 in an England rife with civil discontent, and Clarissa is caught up in events which will alter England's history and lure her into a strange, shadowbox future. First part of a series. Followed by *The Adulteress (RD 19845)*. 1981.

The Bellerose Bargain   RD 18733
by Robyn Carr
narrated by Madelyn Buzzard
4 discs
Set in Restoration England during the boisterous reign of King Charles II. Alicia, a beautiful tavern maid of uncertain parentage, receives a proposal

from Lord Geoffrey asking her to pose as Lady Charlotte, the missing heir to the Bellerose estate. As a sea captain he can then finance his own fleet of ships. Alicia agrees, soon falling in love with the dashing Geoffrey. 1982.

A Duel with Destiny   RD 10938
by Barbara Cartland
narrated by Yolande Baven
2 discs
A young woman is desperately in love with a marquis who wants her as his mistress but not as his wife. 1977.

Love at the Helm   RD 16905
by Barbara Cartland, inspired and helped by Admiral of the Fleet, the Earl Mountbatten of Burma
narrated by Jill Tanner
2 discs
When Captain Horn is ordered to sail to Antigua to deal with American privateers who are attacking British merchant ships, part of his mission is to carry with him the future wife of the governor of Antigua. Horn dislikes having a woman on board in wartime, even more so when she is his cousin and the sister of a man he detests. Nevertheless he is attracted to her. 1981.

Love Locked In   RD 14944
by Barbara Cartland
narrated by Michael McCullough
2 discs
The debauched Duc de Savigne marries a country ingenue who makes him

over into the white knight she knows him to be. 1977.

The Mask of Love   RD 19330
by Barbara Cartland
narrated by Michael McCullough
2 discs
The Marquis of Melford is relieved to be alone at last on his yacht, away from the seductive demands of his dark-eyed mistress and the perpetual merry-making of Venice. He loses both his composure and his solitude, however, when he discovers a fragile, blue-eyed, golden-haired stowaway hiding in his wardrobe. 1975.

Messenger of Love   RD 11999
by Barbara Cartland
narrated by Michael McCullough
2 discs
An unsophisticated young girl is summoned from her father's country estate to serve Queen Elizabeth I at court. It also becomes her duty to be the queen's hidden messenger and uncover a traitor. 1961.

The Naked Battle   RD 13666
by Barbara Cartland
narrated by Yolande Baven
2 discs
After sailing from England to South America with her father, a gun-selling profiteer, Lucilla meets the magnetic rebel leader Bolivar and rescues a mysterious Spanish officer from death. Unknown to Lucilla, she determines the fates of Bolivar's entire army and the man she loves. 1977.

The Outrageous Lady   RD 10988
by Barbara Cartland
narrated by Michael McCullough
2 discs
Young Lady Roysdon lives for adventure, indulging in pranks and practical jokes among the young nobles, until she falls in love with a highwayman. 1977.

The Reluctant Bride   RD 12003
by Barbara Cartland
narrated by Virginia Cromer
3 discs
On her way to meet her future husband, a wealthy prince, Camilla's heart is captured by the handsome Hugo, who appears to despise her for reasons she cannot understand. Not until she finds herself in danger does she learn the startling truth about Hugo's feelings for her. 1972.

The Temptation of Torilla   RD 11004
by Barbara Cartland
narrated by Elizabeth Swain
2 discs
Travelling alone, Torilla and a stranger fall in love on the way to her cousin's wedding, but he turns out to be her cousin's future husband. 1977.

A Touch of Love   RD 11005
by Barbara Cartland
narrated by Christina Gillespie
2 discs
When Tamara Selincourt's sister and brother-in-law are killed, she must take care of her niece and nephew, but she must also turn to a distrusted duke for help. 1977.

Blind Love   RD 8440
by Patrick Cauvin
translated by Elaine P. Halperin
narrated by Livingston Gilbert
2 discs
A shy Parisian professor vacationing in the South of France meets Laura, a beautiful and vivacious blind woman. Their encounter leads to madcap adventures as well as conflicts that threaten to destroy their idyll. Explicit descriptions of sex. 1975.

I Love Miss Tilli Bean   RD 7589
by Ilka Chase
narrated by Ilka Chase
4 discs
The lives of an American girl and her Quaker mother dramatically change when they meet a dashing worldly-wise Italian. Growing up in Italy, Tilli becomes a celebrated beauty but finds happiness only when she returns to America. 1946.

Judith   RD 13704
by Brian Cleeve
narrated by Mitzi Friedlander
5 discs
In nineteenth-century England, young Judith Mortimer, a country bluestocking, is overwhelmed by debts as she cares for her bedridden father and tries to keep their modest estate out of the clutches of the Earl of Matcham. During midnight meetings with a local band of smugglers, Judith

falls in love with Robert Barnabas. Some explicit descriptions of sex. 1978.

Happy All the Time   RD 13129
by Laurie Colwin
narrated by Jim Walton
3 discs
Novel involving four rich young Manhattanites. The story alternates between two romances—the happy marriage of Guido and Holly and the courtship of Misty Berkowitz by Guido's cousin. Some strong language. 1978.

Don't Shut Me Out   RD 13114
by Laura Conway
narrated by Tom Martin
3 discs
In the Bohemian Chelsea section of London at the beginning of the twentieth century, Mab Chalmers, who lives by her wits, does typing for a successful novelist with whom she is in love. A rich, beautiful woman soon captures his heart, but Mab finds someone else. 1974.

Hannah Massey   RD 18242
by Catherine Cookson
narrated by Rachel Gurney
3 discs
Hannah Massey is a fiercely ambitious woman who would use anyone—husband, sons, grandchild, or her daughter Rosie—to gain social acceptability. Rosie is caught between the man she loves and her mother, who hates him. Some strong language. 1964.

Life and Mary Ann   RD 13894
by Catherine Cookson
narrated by Rachel Gurney
3 discs
At seventeen, Mary Ann still loves her childhood sweetheart Corny Boyle. He goes to America, however, apparently leaving the field wide open for Tony, the grandson of Mary Ann's benefactor. Fifth part of an eight-book series. Followed by *Marriage and Mary Ann (RD 13868)*. 1962.

Love and Mary Ann   RD 10741
by Catherine Cookson
narrated by Michael McCullough
2 discs
A country lass with three years of boarding school behind her begins to discover the mystery, wonder, and woes of love. Fourth part of an eight-book series. Followed by *Life and Mary Ann (RD 13894)*. 1976.

The Mallen Lot   RD 8200
by Catherine Cookson
narrated by Pauline Flanagan
4 discs
Continues the saga of the Mallen family during the early 1900s. Focuses on Barbara's illicit love affair and the romances of her children. Last part of a three-book series. Sequel to *The Mallen Girl (RD 6875)*. 1974.

Marriage and Mary Ann   RD 13868
by Catherine Cookson
narrated by Pauline Flanagan
1 disc
Mary Ann Shaughnessy, the irrepress-

ible child of Tyneside, is to marry Corny Boyle, her childhood sweetheart, in five weeks. Everything should be lovely, but few things in life go smoothly for the tempestuous Shaughnessy family. Sixth part of an eight-book series. Followed by *Mary Ann's Angels (RD 13918)*. 1964.

Tilly   RD 15573
by Catherine Cookson
narrated by Michael McCullough
5 discs
During the early reign of Queen Victoria, teenage orphan Tilly Trotter lives with her widowed grandmother, who dies after their place is set afire. Homeless Tilly is hired by mine owner Mark Sopwith to be nursemaid to his four rambunctious children, whom she is able to handle. Later she becomes Mark's housekeeper, and affection grows into love. Some strong language. First part of a three-book series. Followed by *Tilly Wed (RD 15665)*. 1980.

Tilly Alone   RD 17581
by Catherine Cookson
narrated by Michael McCullough
4 discs
Widowed Tilly Trotter, now in her fifties, returns to England with two children after Comanche Indians kill her husband on the Texas frontier. When Tilly sees her childhood sweetheart again after many years, she begins to regret a promise she made her beloved husband on his deathbed. Last

part of a three-book series. Sequel to *Tilly Wed (RD 15665)*. 1982.

Tilly Wed   RD 15665
by Catherine Cookson
narrated by Michael McCullough
5 discs
Continues the saga of love and adversity of the English beauty. Pregnant and with her lover dead, Tilly is spared further persecution from the Sopwith family and the villagers when Mark Sopwith marries her and sweeps her off to Texas. She manages to triumph over the rigors of frontier life, her husband's jealous uncle, and the threats of Indian attacks. Some strong language. Second part of a three-book series. Followed by *Tilly Alone (RD 17581)*. 1981.

**The Chrysanthemum Garden
RD 17588**
by Joseph Cowley
narrated by Pat McDermott
2 discs
Morna Franklin, a fiftyish housewife, married to an insurance agent, walks out of their Scarsdale home after thirty years of marriage when she falls in love with her professor, seventy-year-old poet Denison McCardle, a widower. Death, divorce, and relationships with children remain on the fringes of this autumnal love tale. Some explicit descriptions of sex. 1981.

Elyza RD 10169
by Clare Darcy
narrated by Elizabeth Swain
3 discs
Masquerading as a boy, Elyza Leigh runs away from her London chaperone and the prospect of a dreary marriage. At a country inn, she meets a dashing stranger who befriends her though he is in love with another woman. 1976.

Diana RD 7071
by R. F. Delderfield
narrated by Alan Haines
8 discs
In post-World War II England, a Cockney orphan falls for a willful and wealthy young woman. 1962.

Lavender Lady RD 19832
by Carola Dunn
narrated by Jill Tanner
3 discs
Young David Fairfax, injured on the road, is taken into the Godrics' country home to recuperate. He finds a bustling family of orphaned boys and girls under the care of their sensible half-sister Hester. The love of this London beau for the appealing Hester is temporarily frustrated by the discovery that he is actually the wealthy Earl of Alton. 1983.

Court of Honor RD 12018
by Maria Fagyas
narrated by Edward Blake
1 disc
Young Hungarian noblewoman Alexa marries Hans, a cold, ambitious member of Kaiser Wilhelm's elite guards. Disillusioned by his neglect, she falls in love with the husband of her dead twin sister, whose memory haunts both of them. Some strong language. 1978.

Mayfair RD 12034
by Nancy Fitzgerald
narrated by Mitzi Friedlander
4 discs
Sibilla and Sophia make their social debut in London in the 1850s, as they tour the balls and the great exposition with a series of charming, though marriage-shy, young men. Captures the spirit and conventions of the colorful, aristocratic Victorians. 1978.

Concordia: The Story of Francesca da Rimini, Told by Her Daughter RD 6784
by Frances Fleetwood
narrated by Esther Benson
4 discs
The tragic tale of Paolo and Francesca, lovers from thirteenth-century Italy. Based on a supposed notebook dated 1290 and written by Francesca's daughter, Concordia. 1973.

The Heyday RD 7162
by Bamber Gascoigne
narrated by George Backman
2 discs
An ironic comedy of love set in Britain in the summer of 1905 where

Agnes, an aspiring young actress, joins a Shakespearean troupe. Explicit descriptions of sex. 1973.

I Know My Love   RD 11419
by Catherine Gaskin
narrated by Mitzi Friedlander
5 discs
The story of Adam Langley and the two women who love him—the plain and understanding wife he loves and the beautiful, passionate woman he desires. Set in the Australian goldfields of the 1850s. 1961.

A Most Romantic City   RD 10735
by Mary Ann Gibbs
narrated by Janis Gray
1 disc
Rich widower Charles Pitborough offers marriage to sensible Cecily in exchange for caring for his child and his mansion. 1976.

Ladysmead   RD 19310
by Jane Gillespie
narrated by Rachel Gurney
2 discs
Set in nineteenth-century England. Centers on the Reverend Thomas Lockley and his daughters Sophia and Lucinda, both of whom are resigned to spinsterhood. Sophia's attentions are so focused on coping with interfering nosy neighbors that she does not recognize overtures from attractive would-be swains. 1982.

The Peacock Spring   RD 11857
by Rumer Godden
narrated by Virginia Cromer
3 discs
Sir Edward, a diplomat in New Delhi, sends for his teenage daughters, Una and Hal, who are at a boarding school in England. A crisis arises when sixteen-year-old Una secretly falls in love with a young Indian poet. 1975.

A Season of Delight   RD 18235
by Joanne Greenberg
narrated by Terry Hayes Sales
4 discs
Focuses on a bittersweet year in the life of Grace Dowben, a middle-aged Jewish mother of two grown children, who have left home. Through her work as a volunteer with the town's fire and rescue squad, she realizes that beyond her love for her husband, she is also in love with a young man half her age. Some strong language. 1981.

A Glimpse of Paradise   RD 8285
by Arlene Hale
narrated by Ellen Parks
3 discs
Heather takes on the care of the younger children when her mother dies and her father abandons them. Disillusioned and weary, she doesn't even know how she feels about Shannon or any of the other men who want to marry her. 1974.

Home to the Valley   RD 7405
by Arlene Hale
narrated by Virginia Cromer
2 discs
War-widowed Nicole returns to the valley of her childhood with her young son Todd. Three ardent admirers await her: the man who has always loved her, a lawyer, and the Reverend Aldwin. 1974.

The Other Side of the World   RD 9912
by Arlene Hale
narrated by Shirley Reynolds
3 discs
Vivacious and talented Ann Barker leaves for Hastings Gap upon the death of her favorite uncle, who requested that she spend a year there to inherit the small estate. On her arrival, mysterious events occur as others come forward to claim their share of the inheritance. 1976.

Promise of Tomorrow   RD 6439
by Arlene Hale
narrated by Mitzi Friedlander
2 discs
The aged proprietor of a Florida hotel and her granddaughter Wynne resist the changes of a land boom. Then Wynne finds herself in love with a stranger whose role in the upheaval is a mystery. 1973.

When Love Returns   RD 6529
by Arlene Hale
narrated by Jim Walton
2 discs
A young woman is challenged by running a real estate business until she meets a new man and her life becomes complicated by the return of an old flame. 1970.

Devil's Cub   RD 11252
by Georgette Heyer
narrated by Terry Hayes Sales
4 discs
Mary Challoner practices a deception upon the young Marquis of Vidal when she substitutes herself for her sister. Mary discovers her love for him despite her distrust. 1966.

The Spanish Bride   RD 13087
by Georgette Heyer
narrated by Mitzi Friedlander
6 discs
A young Spanish bride follows her British soldier husband to war during the Napoleonic period. 1978.

The Talisman Ring   RD 13119
by Georgette Heyer
narrated by Tom Martin
3 discs
An unsolved murder mystery, a band of smugglers, and a lost ring are inextricably mixed with the love affairs of a young French girl and her cousins in eighteenth-century England. 1976.

The Street of the City   RD 11007
by Grace Livingston Hill
narrated by Esther Benson
3 discs
The story of Frannie, a charming American girl who lives on the wrong side of the tracks, and a young man

whose friends think she is not good enough for him. A secret shortwave transmitter planted in the cellar of Frannie's home brings matters to a crisis. 1977.

Runaway Bride   RD 8417
by Jane Aiken Hodge
narrated by Dale Carter
3 discs
To avoid marrying an odious fortune hunter, heiress Jennifer Purchas runs away and takes a position as companion to the Duchess of Lewes. She finds herself in an embarrassing predicament when the duchess's grandson shows that she is the object of his affection. 1975.

How Do I Love Thee   RD 9334
by Lucille Iremonger
narrated by Mitzi Friedlander
5 discs
Fictional account of the passionate love affair and happy marriage of the English poets Elizabeth and Robert Browning. 1976.

The Good Husband   RD 14149
by Pamela Hansford Johnson
narrated by Tom Martin
3 discs
During the 1960s in England, a promising young banker marries a somewhat older widow with two young boys. All goes well until he becomes attracted once again to an earlier love. 1978.

Lord Richard's Passion   RD 7692
by Mervyn Jones
narrated by Roy Avers
4 discs
The fortunes of English aristocracy at the turn of the century are interwoven with the doomed romance between Lord Richard and Ellie Comore. Though they become engaged, Ellie believes their love will destroy them and flees to Germany. 1974.

The Children Sing   RD 7144
by MacKinlay Kantor
narrated by Ed Kallay
3 discs
During a guided tour of the Orient, July Lundin steals away from her husband Don for a rendezvous with an old flame in Singapore. 1973.

Late Bloomer   RD 14019
by David A. Kaufelt
narrated by Zoe Corell
3 discs
A sixty-six-year-old widow is genuinely grieving the death of her high-powered husband but is also rather glad of her freedom. She goes to Miami and an "apartmentette" with her wise-cracking pal April, where two very different men compete for her attentions. Some strong language. 1979.

A Gift of Onyx   RD 8250
by Jocelyn Kettle
narrated by Mitzi Friedlander
3 discs
In eighteenth-century England,

More Romances Discs

wealthy and intelligent Eugenie comes to Lancashire as the bride of a country squire whose heart is already filled with love for the country girl who has borne his son. 1974.

Senator Marlowe's Daughter RD 11989
by Frances Parkinson Keyes
narrated by Catherine Byers
6 discs
When the only daughter of a sedate New England senator reluctantly leaves Washington to travel abroad with her mother, she vows to return. Her beauty, charm, and fate lead her through the intrigues of European royalty and romance. 1976.

Steamboat Gothic   RD 16886
by Frances Parkinson Keyes
narrated by Suzanne Toren
10 discs
Chronicles a family through three generations, beginning with the romance of a wealthy reformed professional gambler and a well-born Southern belle. Set in a great plantation house on the Mississippi River in Louisiana from Civil War days until 1930. 1952.

The Moon Tree   RD 14111
by Maud Lang
narrated by Michael McCullough
3 discs
Seventeen-year-old Clem, daughter of a nineteenth-century sheep rancher in New South Wales, is sent to Sydney away from the man she loves. There

at a school for young Presbyterian ladies, she becomes hopelessly entangled with a disreputable artist. 1978.

Summer's Lease   RD 8175
by Celia Larner
narrated by Terry Hayes Sales
3 discs
As a young musician, Jim marries a much older woman for her wealth, maturity, and also for love. His stepdaughter comes to visit at their chateau in France and develops a crush on him. 1974.

For All Your Life   RD 13046
by Emilie Loring
narrated by Catherine Byers
3 discs
A dream-come-true inheritance becomes a nightmare for a lovely career woman. 1977.

Here Comes the Sun   RD 19812
by Emilie Loring
narrated by Janis Gray
3 discs
A hasty marriage plunges Julie into a world of intrigue and heart-rending doubt. 1924.

I Hear Adventure Calling   RD 19810
by Emilie Loring
narrated by Madelyn Buzzard
4 discs
A young heiress finds unexpected romance when her summer vacation turns into a nightmare of fear and suspicion. 1975.

Love with Honor   RD 18227
by Emilie Loring
narrated by Janet Hanson
3 discs
Randi, a secretary, is burdened with the support of her invalid sister. After Randi impulsively marries her rich boss, who is twice her age, she meets the young, handsome love of her life. 1969.

No Time for Love   RD 19044
by Emilie Loring
narrated by Becky Parker
3 discs
Investigating a jewel theft that has clouded her family's good name, Julie is drawn into a world of international intrigue where she meets and falls in love with Mark. He is rich, powerful, and mysterious, with "no time for love." 1970.

The Scottish Marriage   RD 18723
by Karen Lynn
narrated by Ann Hodapp
3 discs
A star-crossed encounter on a stormy Scottish night brings together a helpless, kidnapped orphan and a cocksure rescuer. Compromising circumstances force them to marry—a marriage in name only. Lord Maplethorpe, an honorable man, accepts his fate, but his young bride wants his heart as well as his hand. 1982.

The Flowers of the Forest   RD 15682
by Ruth Doan MacDougall
narrated by Terry Hayes Sales
4 discs
In 1878 Anne and Duncan, both poor Scottish immigrants, marry and move to New Hampshire to start the sheep farm Duncan yearns for. When hard times come upon them in 1901, they take in a schoolteacher as a boarder, and Anne, forty and the mother of six, falls in love with him. 1981.

The Wine of Astonishment   RD 7334
by Rachel MacKenzie
narrated by Esther Benson
2 discs
When their dominating mother dies, Martha and Esther find their lives taking on new meanings. One falls in love with a married man, and the other with their bachelor pastor. 1974.

Castlemore   RD 6819
by Charles Roy Mackinnon
narrated by Tom Martin
5 discs
A turn-of-the-century love affair that rocks the foundation of the Scottish clan living in the great house at Castlemore. 1973.

**When Knighthood Was in Flower
RD 11445**
by Charles Major
narrated by Guy Sorel
4 discs
The story of Charles Brandon and Mary Tudor. In love with Brandon, Mary must obey her brother King

Henry VIII who insists she marry King Louis XII of France. 1970.

Change of Heart   RD 15622
by Sally Mandel
narrated by Esther Benson
4 discs
Twenty-six-year-old Sharlie Converse, born with a defective heart, has always been protected by her self-pitying parents. One day she collapses from the steps of a Madison Avenue bus into the arms of handsome lawyer Brian Morgan. They fall in love, which gives her the courage to undergo a heart transplant operation and the spunk to defy her parents. Some strong language. 1979.

Cardigan Square   RD 11499
by Alexandra Manners
narrated by Dale Carter
4 discs
In nineteenth-century England, a farmer's daughter becomes Lady Agatha's companion. Two fiercely handsome brothers are rivals for her affection. 1977.

The Slow Awakening   RD 13932
by Catherine Marchant
narrated by Meg Wynn-Owen
4 discs
In rural England in 1850, Kirston McGregor, a spirited orphan of mysterious origin, is rescued by a servant of the wealthy Knutsson family after a flood sweeps the countryside. In their household she bears a child, is given a job, and learns of the loveless mar-

riage between the master and his bride. 1976.

The Liaison   RD 10208
by Maria Matray and Answald Kruger
translated by Richard Sharp
narrated by Suzanne Toren
5 discs
One of the great untold royal love stories as seen through the diaries of the lovers, Princess Louise of Coburg and Lieutenant Geza von Mattachich. The diaries were discovered by a journalist in an antique store in Budapest. 1975.

Chance the Winds of Fortune
RD 15617
by Laurie McBain
narrated by Michael Clarke-Laurence
7 discs
Fortune smiles on Dante Leighton, titled lord turned pirate. Sailing before the Sea Dragon's towering mast, he plunders hearts and cargos from the Carolinas to Trinidad's turquoise lagoons. When a series of dazzling intrigues results in the abduction of golden-haired Rhea, her fate converges with his in a quest for sunken Spanish treasure. First part of a series. Followed by *Dark before the Rising Sun (RD 18240)*. 1980.

**Dark before the Rising Sun
RD 18240**
by Laurie McBain
narrated by Norman Barrs
7 discs
The love affair of Lady Rhea Claire and her titled-lord-turned-pirate lover, Captain Dante Leighton, during the eighteenth century. Sailing from the West Indies, they return to Dante's ancestral estate in England, where the memories of the past and the turmoil of the present severely test their love. Descriptions of sex. Second part of a series. Sequel to *Chance the Winds of Fortune (RD 15617).* Bestseller. 1982.

Maggie Royal   RD 17218
by Jane McIlvaine McClary
narrated by Barbara Caruso
7 discs
Maggie Royal and Jared Stark grow up together in love on an idyllic, unspoiled island off the coast of Georgia. Fate causes them to go their separate ways, but they meet again in war-time London, where their childhood love is rekindled. 1981.

Ayisha   RD 6148
by Helen Noga
narrated by Mitzi Friedlander
2 discs
Caught in a clash between Armenians and Turks in the early part of this century, Ayisha falls in love with the handsome Bayazid, who saves her from a barbaric fate. 1972.

Come Back to Me, Beloved   RD 15522
by Kathleen Norris
narrated by Janis Gray
1 disc
Eighteen-year-old Maryls Hazeltine, who lives in California, falls in love at first sight with a former Yale man ten years her senior. Meanwhile her father, who is a judge, fights a blackmail attempt by his opposition during his run for the U.S. Senate. 1942.

Maiden Voyage   RD 15521
by Kathleen Norris
narrated by Mitzi Friedlander
4 discs
Tony, a San Francisco society reporter, discovers that romance is more than news for her column when she falls in love with her best friend's husband. 1934.

Trumpet for a Walled City   RD 9342
by Dolores Pala
narrated by Mitzi Friedlander
4 discs
Old-fashioned love story between Eileen O'Donovan, a young American journalist living in Paris, and Shannon Cavanaugh, a noted film star. 1974.

The Magic Ship   RD 14142
by Sandra Paretti
translated by Ruth Hein
narrated by George Guidall
4 discs
During the summer season on the United States Eastern seaboard, the captain and crew of a German luxury liner, "Cecile," suddenly find them-

selves stranded off Bar Harbor, Maine, with the sudden outbreak of World War I in Europe. The liner remains offshore while romances blossom and endearing memories are forged among the crew and people at Bar Harbor. 1979.

Under Gemini   RD 10260
by Rosamunde Pilcher
narrated by Lee Johns
4 discs
Flora and Rose, identical twins separated from birth, meet twenty years later. Rose convinces Flora to act as her stand-in for a visit to her fiance's grandmother, and Flora finds intrigue, suspense, and romance on the journey. 1976.

Gay Lord Robert   RD 10015
by Jean Plaidy
narrated by George Patterson
4 discs
Robert Dudley and Elizabeth I were passionate lovers who might have married but for the existence of Robert's tragic young wife. 1955.

Magic Garden   RD 19538
by Gene Stratton-Porter
narrated by John Stratton
2 discs
An old-fashioned romance that flowers when Amaryllis and John are children. John introduces her to the magic garden where they first pledge their love. 1976.

White Fawn   RD 18188
by Olive Higgins Prouty
narrated by Michael McCullough
4 discs
Story of a wealthy young girl, innocent in the ways of love but hungry for her right to happiness, and a struggling young doctor. They discover too late the fate of lovers who oppose the very rich. 1931.

Gentle Greaves   RD 6088
by Ernest Raymond
narrated by Burt Blackwell
9 discs
In Victorian England, two cousins who had been lovers but married others meet years later and resume their passionate affair. 1972.

The Old June Weather   RD 7613
by Ernest Raymond
narrated by Milton Metz
3 discs
Concerns an old and great love as it was lived a century ago and as it was discovered by two teenagers, Travers Ibraham and Gael Harrington, almost half a century later. 1957.

Paddington Green   RD 9553
by Claire Rayner
narrated by Ada Brown Mather
5 discs
Set in Victorian London. Focuses on an aging surgeon patriarch and his daughter, a young widow, whose love for a Sephardic Jew is forbidden by tradition and his faith. Third part of a

series. Sequel to *The Haymarket (RD 7503)*. 1975.

Buttes Landing   RD 6600
by Jean Rikhoff
narrated by Gordon Gould
6 discs
A stubborn individualist settles in a remote corner of the Adirondack region of New York to farm and meets a young woman who begins to teach him about love and humanity. 1973.

Wicked Loving Lies   RD 10223
by Rosemary Rogers
narrated by Mitzi Friedlander
8 discs
Centers on Marisa, the goddaughter of Napoleon's first wife Josephine, whose life begins in a sheltered convent. From there she progresses to the intrigues of Napoleon's court, undergoes captivity in a Turkish harem, and is sold as a slave in Louisiana. Explicit descriptions of sex. 1976.

Rhine Journey   RD 17271
by Ann Schlee
narrated by Rachel Gurney
2 discs
A nineteenth-century English spinster taking a Rhine steamer trip with her relatives meets a man who reminds her of her one youthful love. The ensuing emotional tensions come into sharp contrast with her staid and melancholy existence, and she takes the first faltering steps to redefine her life and her relationships with others. 1980.

Doctor's Destiny   RD 15469
by Elizabeth Seifert
narrated by Janis Gray
3 discs
Dr. Storm Linders knows exactly what he wants: a surgical practice in his grandfather's hospital and marriage to faithful Kathryn. Then he visits an old friend in Bayard and agrees to stay on for a little while at Bayard Hospital, where Mary Ruble, part of the operating team, is everything Kathryn is not. Storm has to reevaluate his whole future. 1972.

Foxfire   RD 9560
by Anya Seton
narrated by Barbara Caruso
5 discs
Amanda Lawrence of New York is on her way home from Europe when she meets, falls in love with, and marries handsome Jonathan Dartland, part Apache and a mining engineer. Unhappy in the bleak little town of Lodestone, Arizona, Amanda dreams of great wealth when she finds a map to a lost gold mine. 1975.

The Cannaway Concern   RD 15549
by Graham Shelby
narrated by Norman Barrs
4 discs
In eighteenth-century England, the defiant young daughter of Brydd and Elizabeth Cannaway elopes with courtly Brook Wintersill. She soon discovers that her life is endangered by his brutality and leaves for her parents' home, where Brook follows with

his ruffian companions. Charlotte escapes once again and falls in love with Jacobite Captain Matcham Lodge. Some violence and some strong language. Second part of a series. Sequel to *The Cannaways (RD 11233)*. 1980.

The Cannaways   RD 11233
by Graham Shelby
narrated by George Backman
4 discs
Brydd Cannaway, whose success as a carriage maker has taken him from poverty to fabulous wealth, becomes involved in a tragic love affair with his childhood sweetheart in Wiltshire. Some explicit descriptions of sex. First of a series. Followed by *The Cannaway Concern (RD 15549)*. 1978.

My Lady Hoyden   RD 17578
by Lane Sheridan
narrated by Michael McCullough
5 discs
Set in the Victorian period. Follows the loves and fortunes of Amanda, a spirited beauty who earns a "reputation" for an innocent dalliance with the visiting Prince of Wales. Married to a grossly unsuitable blueblood, Amanda languishes until she falls in love with her dashing brother-in-law. 1981.

The Maclarens   RD 13011
by C. L. Skelton
narrated by Burt Blackwell
4 discs
Andrew Maclaren, the future commander of the Scottish 148th Regiment of Foot involved in nineteenth-century skirmishes in China and India, returns from his first battle with a lovely survivor. He finds that the stuffiness of military society, including his parents, prohibits their union. Some strong language. 1978.

The Catherine Wheel   RD 17288
by Jean Stafford
narrated by Michael McCullough
3 discs
In a small New England town near Boston, Katharine Congreve becomes enmeshed in the lives of her cousin Maeve and John Shipley, the man whom Maeve marries and Katharine has secretly loved. 1951.

Loving   RD 15642
by Danielle Steel
narrated by Michael McCullough
4 discs
The nineteen-year-old daughter of a successful but imprudent author has everything her father's money can buy. After he dies, leaving her penniless, she samples four husbands in her search for the love she has never known. 1980.

The Promise   RD 15486
by Danielle Steel, based on a screenplay by Garry Michael White
narrated by John Stratton
3 discs
Michael and Nancy are two young lovers who are determined to marry despite the objections of Michael's strong-willed mother. However, on

the day of their wedding a tragic automobile accident results in a severe test of their promise never to say goodbye to each other. Some strong language. 1978.

Summer's End   RD 18252
by Danielle Steel
narrated by Barbara Caruso
4 discs
After a lonely twenty-year marriage between Deanna and her French husband Marc cools, she retreats to her painting and their only child, Pilar. By chance Deanna meets a gallery owner who takes an interest in her work, and the two fall in love. 1979.

Anna and Her Daughters   RD 14089
by D. E. Stevenson
narrated by Michael McCullough
3 discs
After the death of her husband, Anna Harcourt finds herself in financial straits. She sells their fine old house, leaves her comfortable life in London, and moves to Scotland with her three daughters, where they find work and romance. 1958.

The Baker's Daughter   RD 10157
by D. E. Stevenson
narrated by Pat Gilbert-Read
3 discs
Unhappy with her dour father and new stepmother, Sue accepts a job as housekeeper for an English artist and his wife, recent arrivals in the small Scottish village. When the artist's wife leaves him, Sue stays on. 1938.

Bel Lamington   RD 15148
by D. E. Stevenson
narrated by Terry Hayes Sales
3 discs
Orphaned and brought up in an English village, shy Bel has to earn a living as a secretary in London. On holiday at a fishing hotel in Scotland, she meets some delightful characters. First part of a series. Followed by *Fletcher's End (RD 14947)*. 1961.

The English Air   RD 9547
by D. E. Stevenson
narrated by Dale Carter
3 discs
Set in the English countryside during the first frenzied months of World War II. Franz von Heiden, son of a high Nazi official and an English mother who died when he was a child, falls in love with Wynne Braithwaite. 1976.

Fletcher's End   RD 14947
by D. E. Stevenson
narrated by Janis Gray
4 discs
Tells of Bel's marriage to Ellis Brownlee, a partner in a firm that owns large warehouses at the Pool of London. They buy Fletcher's End, a house that had belonged to the late Miss Lestrange. Her personality was so strong that it is still influencing people's lives, for good or ill. Second part of a series. Sequel to *Bel Lamington (RD 15148)*. 1962.

More Romances Discs

Smouldering Fire   RD 6506
by D. E. Stevenson
narrated by Andy Chappell
4 discs
Iain MacAslan rents his Scottish estate to a wealthy Londoner who brings up a large house party for the shooting and fishing seasons. Among the guests is Margaret, the woman Iain loved years before. 1966.

Spring Magic   RD 14088
by D. E. Stevenson
narrated by Michael McCullough
4 discs
A shy, retiring, young Englishwoman spends her early years in the home of a selfish aunt. At twenty-five something happens to change the course of her life—a bomb lands in the London square near her aunt's house. When her aunt departs for the South of England, Frances escapes to a quiet village on the coast of Scotland, where a new existence awaits her. 1974.

Wildfire at Midnight   RD 11859
by Mary Stewart
narrated by Dale Carter
3 discs
Gianetta Brooke travels to a remote island in Scotland to try to forget the husband she divorced. There in the mountains she comes face-to-face with a murderer and renews her relationship with her former husband. 1956.

Strathmore   RD 10183
by Jessica Stirling
narrated by Dale Carter
3 discs
A young woman in a Scottish mining town in 1875 finds herself torn between loyalty to her family and class and her forbidden love for the married owner of the mines. 1975.

From This Day Forward   RD 17508
by Elswyth Thane
narrated by Jacqueline Coslow
5 discs
The marriage between a famous ornithologist and a beautiful dancer is jeopardized by diverging interests and careers. 1941.

Letter to a Stranger   RD 6236
by Elswyth Thane
narrated by Terry Hayes Sales
2 discs
A warm-hearted novelist tries to help a fan-mail correspondent and finds herself involved in some unforeseen romance. 1954.

The Lost General   RD 15561
by Elswyth Thane
narrated by Janis Gray
3 discs
The general has been dead for a hundred and seventy years, but Mary Carmichael falls in love with him. When she goes South to trace down everything possible about his life and death, she meets a modern young soldier who brings romance into her world. 1953.

The Duke's Daughter   RD 11915
by Angela Thirkell
narrated by Elizabeth Swain
5 discs
Set in the fictional English county of Barsetshire. The flirtatious and beautiful Lady Pallesen is tugged toward the altar by a man she does not want and is ignored by a man she yearns for. 1973.

The Headmistress   RD 6005
by Angela Thirkell
narrated by Terry Hayes Sales
4 discs
Madeline Sparling becomes headmistress of a girls' school and has great plans for the school and her life. Then she meets two dignified gentlemen who are romantically inclined. 1972.

Jutland Cottage   RD 13205
by Angela Thirkell
narrated by Carmen Mathews
4 discs
In Barsetshire, Margot Phelps, the selfless, overworked, middle-aged daughter of Admiral Phelps, has given her whole life to taking care of her aging parents. One day, however, the beautiful and blundering Rose Fairweather introduces Margot to Mr. Macfadyen, who discovers her attractions. 1953.

The Two Bishops   RD 15676
by Agnes Sligh Turnbull
narrated by John Stratton
4 discs
Focuses on Cissie, a talented pianist,

who enters into the lives of recently retired Bishop Ware and his successor Bishop Armstrong. Cissie lays siege to the young bishop's heart and helps him resolve the anguish of a private vow of celibacy. 1980.

The Mixed Blessing   RD 13153
by Helen Van Slyke
narrated by John Stratton
6 discs
A gentle and courageous young woman, the child of a racially mixed marriage, is torn between her passion for the one man she desperately loves and loyalty to her family. Sequel to *The Heart Listens (RD 7337)*. 1975.

Runaway Girl   RD 13020
by Lucy Walker
narrated by Jill Tanner
3 discs
Headstrong Jenny wants more out of life than a husband and more in a husband than the man her father wants her to marry. To escape her fate, she runs away to the opal mines and goldfields of the Australian outback, only to discover that she can't run away from love. 1975.

So Much Love   RD 12024
by Lucy Walker
narrated by Michael McCullough
3 discs
Nairee, an orphan raised by a kindly old woman in the outback of Australia, returns home from college and falls in love with two very different men. 1977.

Columbella   RD 11498
by Phyllis A. Whitney
narrated by Dale Carter
4 discs
Mystery set in the Virgin Islands which pits two women against each other for a man, a child, and their very lives. 1966.

The Fire and the Gold   RD 13050
by Phyllis A. Whitney
narrated by Lois Smith
2 discs
On the day that Melora returns to San Francisco, a violent earthquake turns her comfortable world and home into ruins. Although she was engaged to handsome Quent of Nob Hill, she meets an impetuous young man who plunges her into romantic conflict. 1974.

Skye Cameron   RD 9933
by Phyllis A. Whitney
narrated by Mitzi Friedlander
4 discs
In New Orleans of 1880, Skye Cameron, daughter of a Scottish father and a Creole mother, considers herself plain until she meets Justin Law. 1957.

Cassettes

After   RC 16201
by Robert Anderson
narrated by Grace Ragsdale
2 cassettes
After his wife dies of cancer, Chris Larsen rediscovers passion with a young actress and probes his feelings about love and desire. Explicit descriptions of sex. 1973.

Adam's Eden   RC 11530
by Faith Baldwin
narrated by John Stratton
1 cassette
When the roving, cosmopolitan Adam Steele decides to settle in a picturesque New England town, no one is more surprised than his self-reliant grandmother. She and her indestructible spirit help him to discover his true self and a lasting romance. 1977.

The Golden Shoestring   RC 11659
by Faith Baldwin
narrated by Janis Gray
2 cassettes
Two young people each think the other is wealthy. How long can they maintain their pretense—and their love—living on hospitality and a golden shoestring? 1974.

He Married a Doctor   RC 18899
by Faith Baldwin
narrated by Rosemary Schwartzel
2 cassettes
Story of a doctor torn between the responsibilities of her medical career and the demands of her marriage. At first her husband seems to understand how important medicine is to her, but later he is tempted by the charms of another woman, who is prepared to devote all her time to him. 1944.

You and Me, Babe RC 8023
by Chuck Barris
narrated by Richard Harmel
3 cassettes
Tommy Christin, son of a Queens chiropodist, and Samantha Wilkerson, daughter of a rich Connecticut family, marry and romp their way through America and Europe until love goes wrong. Strong language. Bestseller. 1974.

Love for Lydia RC 15439
by H. E. Bates
narrated by Merwin Smith
2 cassettes
Characterization of a young girl developing from shy awkwardness to bold certainty in her relations with men. The story, set in the 1920s in England, is told by one of the four men whom she influences most deeply— the one whom she first chooses as her lover and turns to again after two others have died. Also issued on flexible disc as FD 15439. 1952.

Odette RC 7866
by Reuben Bercovitch
narrated by Ann Pugh
3 cassettes
Promised to a Massachusetts man by a mail-order marriage arranged by her father, Odette experiences humiliation, is captured by the Apaches, and finds unexpected love. Based on letters discovered in the Department of the Interior files. 1973.

The Book of Eve RC 8697
by Constance Beresford-Howe
narrated by Mary Jane Higby
3 cassettes
Married to a cranky invalid for forty years, Eve leaves her husband to start life again. She falls in love with a crazy Hungarian half her age and gets reborn. 1973.

A Matter of Feeling RC 16316
by Janine Boissard
translated by Elizabeth Walter
narrated by Patricia Beaudry
2 cassettes
Events of a winter and spring in the life of the Moreau family, who have a happy, comfortable home outside Paris. Centers on seventeen-year-old Pauline, who hopes to be a writer, and her bittersweet romance with Pierre, a forty-year-old Parisian artist. Some strong language. 1979.

Tickets RC 18842
by Richard P. Brickner
narrated by Jack Hrkach
2 cassettes
During intermission at the Metropolitan Opera, a debonair bachelor meets an enchanting married woman. Believing that life is full of significant surprises and as melodramatic as opera, the bachelor attempts to orchestrate their subsequent affair as he imagines it should be written, but the lovers are soon playing out their romance for real. Some strong language and explicit descriptions of sex. 1981.

More Romances Cassettes

Open Heart   RC 18884
by Mary Bringle
narrated by Sally Darling
3 cassettes
Rafaella Leone, a young Italian widow, arrives at the famed Houston Medical Center for cardiovascular surgery by world-renowned Dr. Lassiter. Before her operation, she meets documentary filmmaker Stephen Morrissey, who befriends her and becomes her lover. Some strong language and some descriptions of sex. 1982.

Lucy Emmett; Or, A Lady of Quality   RC 12820
by Anita Bronson
narrated by Yolande Baven
3 cassettes
The love child of farmer Roger Emmett and a gypsy beauty, Lucy Emmett catches the eye of Squire Royalston and is whisked away to become schooled in the courtly arts. She falls in love with the Earl of Lansdun and devises a bold and reckless scheme to win him for her own. Some strong language and some explicit descriptions of sex. 1978.

Come, My Beloved   RC 11835
by Pearl S. Buck
narrated by Suzanne Toren
2 cassettes
Livy is the fourth generation of her American family living in India. She falls in love with an Indian doctor. When she wants to marry him, her missionary father refuses to grant permission. 1953.

East Wind, West Wind   RC 11914
by Pearl S. Buck
narrated by Jeanne Hopson
1 cassette
The daughter of a noble Chinese family, trained for wifehood in the old customs, is married to a man of the new era who received his medical education in America. She finds happiness and love only when she adopts Western habits. 1930.

Peony   RC 9091
by Pearl S. Buck
narrated by Marie Pearsall
5 cassettes
Set in nineteenth-century China. Peony, Chinese bondmaid of a rich Jewish family, has always loved David, the family's only son. Because tradition forbids their love, Peony sublimates her passion, vowing to choose the best bride for David and to serve him as long as he will have her. 1948.

Wait until Evening   RC 8620
by Henrietta Buckmaster
narrated by Gillian Wilson
3 cassettes
Terror-stricken and alone after an auto accident, Catherine Mills, just arrived in England from the United States, finds shelter with Axel Lund, a scientist staying at a nearby farmhouse. 1974.

The Alleys of Eden   RC 18902
by Robert Olen Butler
narrated by Dick Jenkins
2 cassettes
An American deserter in Vietnam falls in love with a bargirl in Saigon, where they live in blissful but threatened secrecy for many years. When Saigon falls, the two flee to the United States, but their future is threatened by the clash of cultures and his continued status as a fugitive. Strong language and some descriptions of sex. 1981.

Any Two Can Play   RC 15858
by Elizabeth Cadell
narrated by Michael McCullough
1 cassette
Twenty-seven-year-old Natalie Travers takes it upon herself to rescue her brother from domestic chaos and taking care of twins when his wife leaves him. Independent and happily unmarried, she feels disinclined to change her status until romance unexpectedly appears in the shape of Henry Downing, scion of the town's founding family. Also issued on flexible disc as FD 15858. 1981.

The Marrying Kind   RC 15776
by Elizabeth Cadell
narrated by Terry Hayes Sales
2 cassettes
Neither Jess Seton, impulsive, impatient, and besieged by men, nor her easy-going, old-fashioned sister Laura are the marrying type. Their happy, independent lives are jolted when

their father gets himself into trouble in Paris, and the sisters seek to help him. 1980.

Parson's House   RC 14637
by Elizabeth Cadell
narrated by Tom Martin
2 cassettes
Divorced, Jeanne Brisson returns with her four-year-old twin daughters to Parson's House, a retreat on the English coast that she had visited happily ten years earlier. But strange rumors have grown up around the old house and a series of "accidents" lead to unexpected developments, the most surprising of which will be the discovery of a real love. 1977.

Return Match   RC 13815
by Elizabeth Cadell
narrated by Debbie Trissell
2 cassettes
Back from Brazil to work in London, international playboy Nigel Pressley finds that Rona, his mother's goddaughter, is an ugly duckling turned swan. Rona, however, seems determined to spurn Nigel's overtures until some visitors stir up an old tragedy with sinister aspects. Also issued on flexible disc as FD 13815. 1979.

The Round Dozen   RC 12318
by Elizabeth Cadell
narrated by Jill Ferris
2 cassettes
In London, a rich bachelor is tracking down a priceless family heirloom missing since 1702. His sleuthing leads

him into the rural countryside where he meets the Cambridgeshire secretary who not only helps him find the missing antique, but ends his search for the perfect woman. Also issued on flexible disc as FD 12318. 1978.

The Dragon and the Pearl   RC 12150
by Barbara Cartland
narrated by Elizabeth Swain
1 cassette
Major Stanton Ware, the prime minister's informant on a dangerous mission to Peking during the Boxer Rebellion, is astounded to discover that his companion in espionage is the most beautiful girl he has ever seen. 1977.

Flowers for the God of Love   RC 14352
by Barbara Cartland
narrated by Michael McCullough
1 cassette
Dashing adventurer and secret agent Rex Davoit cannot afford to go to India as lieutenant governor of the Northwest Province to spy on the Russians unless he marries rich, beautiful, but icy, Quenella. 1979.

The Ghost Who Fell in Love   RC 13832
by Barbara Cartland
narrated by Jill Ferris
1 cassette
Set in 1822 during the Royal Race Week at Ascot. A young girl is hidden by her brother in the secret priest's room of the manor house now rented out to a dashing earl. Smitten by the handsome nobleman, she pre-

tends she is a ghost and warns her beloved of the plots she overhears against him. Also issued on flexible disc as FD 13832. 1978.

Journey to Paradise   RC 16299
by Barbara Cartland
narrated by Bets Thompson
2 cassettes
In 1839 Kamala Lindsey, an orphan, runs away when she is told by her hateful uncle that he is going to force her to marry a man of sixty. Intending to seek a new life in France, Kamala is involved in an accident with a handsome young stranger and nurses him back to health. 1974.

The Judgement of Love   RC 14588
by Barbara Cartland
narrated by Janis Gray
1 cassette
A young heiress visits her guardian's English estate. There she is introduced to his three nephews, in hopes she will marry one. 1978.

Love for Sale   RC 15827
by Barbara Cartland
narrated by Jill Ferris
1 cassette
When Udela Hayward's father dies, Lord Julius Westry offers her employment in London. Delighted at first, she soon realizes that the destination of the carriage sent to meet her is a brothel. She runs away into the arms of the Duke of Westry, the brother of the rakish lord. Also issued on flexible disc as FD 15827. 1980.

Love in the Clouds RC 16116
by Barbara Cartland
narrated by Hazel Kiley
1 cassette
Chandra Wardell's father, a famous Sanskrit scholar, is commissioned by Lord Frome to accompany him to Nepal. When the eminent professor suffers a heart attack, Chandra, who has helped her father for many years, goes in his place. On her arrival she encounters the anger of woman-hating Frome, but their antipathy to each other lessens when they discover a sacred manuscript and become involved in danger. 1979.

Love Leaves at Midnight RC 16240
by Barbara Cartland
narrated by Sandy Nelson
1 cassette
On a lark, Xenia and her look-alike cousin, whose mothers were identical twins, switch places to see how their boyfriends will react. The exchange causes numerous romantic complications. 1978.

The Love Pirate RC 11537
by Barbara Cartland
narrated by Yolande Baven
1 cassette
Bertilla Alvinston's mother sends her to Sarawak as a missionary to get her away from home. After many adventures, Bertilla falls in love with trade investigator Lord Saire. 1977.

The Passion and the Flower RC 12391
by Barbara Cartland
narrated by Yvonne Fair Tessler
1 cassette
All of Paris tries to meet Lokita, the secretive young ballet dancer. Prince Volkonski, on holiday from the Tsarist court, succeeds—but only briefly. A protective duenna, the prince's blue blood, and Lokita's mysterious background are obstacles to the couple's happiness. Also issued on flexible disc as FD 12391. 1978.

A Princess in Distress RC 13225
by Barbara Cartland
narrated by Martha Thrush
1 cassette
At Marienbad, Lord Arkley meets and falls in love with Marisha, wife of the drunken and crippled Prince Friederich, who plans to use her as a political spy. 1978.

The Problems of Love RC 13643
by Barbara Cartland
narrated by Diane Eilenberg
1 cassette
Alexia and her younger sister come to London for their debutante season. They seek the aid of their distant cousin, the self-centered Marquis of Osminton, in meeting the right people. Also issued on flexible disc as FD 13643. 1978.

The Wild, Unwilling Wife   RC 13259
by Barbara Cartland
narrated by Elizabeth Swain
1 cassette
In 1825 Alvaric Verne returns to England from an African safari to assume his title as the eleventh Lord Verhnam, only to find the estate mortgaged to Muir, a wealthy neighbor. Verhnam is told that the property will be returned to him on condition that he marry Muir's daughter. 1977.

Dear Intruder   RC 11328
by Ilka Chase
narrated by Ilka Chase
2 cassettes
A good-looking, happily married grandmother in her sixties has an affair with an old British friend. Some strong language. 1976.

Sally Hemings   RC 13990
by Barbara Chase-Riboud
narrated by Yvonne Tessler
3 cassettes
A speculative, fictional account of a love story between Thomas Jefferson and a slave mistress with whom he lived for thirty-eight years until his death. Sally Hemings had seven children, all of whom were said to be fathered by Jefferson. Some strong language. Also issued on flexible disc as FD 13990. 1979.

The Blind Miller   RC 19637
by Catherine Cookson
narrated by Dayle Malina
2 cassettes
Young Sarah feels grateful to David, the husband who lifted her from working-class squalor by marrying her. But she feels reckless passion for his handsome, willful brother, who has dominated David his whole life long. 1963.

The Cinder Path   RC 12487
by Catherine Cookson
narrated by George Patterson
2 cassettes
Charlie MacFell travels from a rural boyhood in Edwardian England to the trenches of World War I before he finds himself. Married to the wrong woman and traumatized by war, he finally achieves self-liberation through reunion with a first love. 1978.

The Dwelling Place   RC 15114
by Catherine Cookson
narrated by Meg Wynn-Owen
3 cassettes
Set in England in the 1840s. Cissie, an orphan who must care for her nine brothers and sisters, has a baby by the local lord's son. She is forced to relinquish her child to save her sister from imprisonment. 1971.

The Girl   RC 10840
by Catherine Cookson
narrated by Yvonne Fair Tessler
2 cassettes
Trapped by her illegitimate birth and

abused by her mistress, at sixteen the plucky heroine submits to an unhappy marriage. Somehow she survives and eventually finds her heart's desire. Also issued on flexible disc as FD 10840. 1977.

The Invitation   RC 8544
by Catherine Cookson
narrated by Patricia Beaudry
4 cassettes
Though Maggie is enthralled by her handsome new husband and his dynamic business success, she discovers a shameful secret in his life that threatens their marriage. 1974.

Miss Martha Mary Crawford RC 16485
by Catherine Cookson
narrated by Azaleigh Maginnis
2 cassettes
Nineteenth-century English tale about a young woman who must help the family survive after her widowed father's death. When she discovers that his money was squandered on a mistress, she is given moral support by a young doctor. 1976.

The Round Tower   RC 19891
by Catherine Cookson
narrated by Mary Woods
2 cassettes
Wealthy Vanessa Ratcliffe, pregnant with another man's child, marries Angus Cotton, the ambitious son of a servant. Vanessa defies her father to marry Angus, and all too soon conflict and doubt begin to nag at the newlyweds. 1975.

Breakaway   RC 10791
by Louise Field Cooper
narrated by Flo Gibson
2 cassettes
When a sixty-year-old widow receives a visit from a garrulous brother who appears to have no intention of leaving, she sets out to see the world on her own. In France she meets a retired civil engineer and suddenly is happier than ever. 1977.

A Pocketful of Rye   RC 12849
by A. J. Cronin
narrated by Hal Tenny
1 cassette
A young British doctor weary of working with the poor secures a pleasant job for himself in a Swiss clinic. To the clinic comes widowed Cathy, his first love, with her ill son Daniel. Daniel becomes the focus of a startling revelation. 1969.

Night Way   RC 17420
by Janet Dailey
narrated by Mitzi Friedlander
3 cassettes
Launa Marshall, a young nurse, becomes involved in the passionate clash between Chad Faulkner and his half-breed brother, Hawk, both the sons of a rich Arizona landowner. Strong language and explicit descriptions of sex. 1981.

Ride the Thunder   RC 16589
by Janet Dailey
narrated by Jack Hrkach
2 cassettes
A glamorous New York socialite on a hunting party out West meets a rugged stranger whose fiery touch sparks her passion. Their romantic idyll is shattered by a terrible secret that claims one life and threatens to destroy another. Some strong language. Also issued on flexible disc as FD 16589. 1980.

Stands a Calder Man   RC 18693
by Janet Dailey
narrated by Yvonne Fair Tessler
3 cassettes
Webb Calder is used to fighting man and nature to get what he wants. When homesteaders flock to Montana to seize their share of the American dream and incidentally, to cramp the Calders' style, Webb finds among them the only woman he has ever wanted. Third part of a series. Sequel to *This Calder Sky (RC 17306)*. Also issued on flexible disc as FD 18693. Bestseller. 1983.

This Calder Range   RC 17714
by Janet Dailey
narrated by Yvonne Fair Tessler
3 cassettes
Story of a determined young rancher and the beautiful but practical bride who rides beside him to the Montana range. Old grudges and debts follow the settlers into the new land as they breathe life into a dream of freedom and a promise of riches. First part of a series. Followed by *This Calder Sky (RC 17306)*. Some explicit descriptions of sex. Also issued on flexible disc as FD 17714. Bestseller. 1982.

This Calder Sky   RC 17306
by Janet Dailey
narrated by Yvonne Fair Tessler
3 cassettes
The great Calder empire stretches across the Montana plains as far as the eye can see. Everyone knows a Calder's word is law, and that one day Chase Calder will take the reins of power and carry the name to new glories. But for handsome, arrogant Chase there is also beautiful, headstrong Maggie O'Rourke, who is determined to be free of harsh codes. Second part of a series. Followed by *Stands a Calder Man (RC 18693)*. Also issued on flexible disc as FD 17306. Bestseller. 1981.

Touch the Wind   RC 17162
by Janet Dailey
narrated by Mitzi Friedlander
2 cassettes
Sheila, a wealthy college student from Texas, elopes to Mexico with her arrogant, golddigger boyfriend. When their car breaks down and a group of bandits kill her husband, the rugged and ruthless leader, Rafaga, takes her as his prisoner and mistress. 1979.

The Tiger's Woman   RC 17193
by Celeste de Blasis
narrated by Catherine Byers
4 cassettes
In 1869, a dancing girl fleeing from a dangerous past comes to San Francisco, where she meets the Tiger, a man who has vast shipping and logging interests. She agrees to be his mistress in return for his protection. But as their love grows, the past catches up with them and they face a difficult test. Explicit descriptions of sex. 1981.

Mary Wakefield   RC 18924
by Mazo de la Roche
narrated by Laura Giannarelli
2 cassettes
A young Englishwoman is hired by Ernest Whiteoak to be governess to Philip's motherless children. When Philip falls in love with her, his mother does all she can to prevent the marriage. Third part of a sixteen-book series. Followed by *Young Renny (RC 11182)*. 1973.

Renny's Daughter   RC 9615
by Mazo de la Roche
narrated by Priscilla Husserl
4 cassettes
Renny's daughter travels to Ireland and becomes involved in a frustrating romance. Fourteenth part of a sixteen-book series. Followed by *Variable Winds at Jalna (RC 18762)*. 1951.

The Realms of Gold   RC 9476
by Margaret Drabble
narrated by Dale Carter
3 cassettes
A divorced mother of four, Frances Wingate is a famous archaeologist in love with a distinguished scholar who is married. Some strong language. 1975.

Countess   RC 12979
by Josephine Edgar
narrated by Meg Wynn-Owen
3 cassettes
Viola from London lives in luxury in pre-war Vienna with her husband, their three children, and James-Carlo, the beloved child of her love affair with Lord Staffray. Her world collapses when her husband is killed in the war and she is pursued by a ruthless prince. 1978.

Chelsea   RC 16576
by Nancy Fitzgerald
narrated by Michael McCullough
2 cassettes
A frothy Victorian novel about the romance of a portrait painter and his model, an orphaned nursemaid. The comedy and fluttery complications are provided by a failing cast-iron furniture business named Fluster and Muddle and characters that include Veracity Flutterby and a titled lady and her marriageable daughter. 1979.

Zemindar   RC 17707
by Valerie Fitzgerald
narrated by Jill Ferris
6 cassettes
Laura Hewitt sails with cousin Emily
and Charles on their wedding trip to
Lucknow, India. Charles's brother
Oliver falls in love with Laura shortly
before the infamous Sepoy Rebellion
of 1857 engulfs them all in danger and
violence. Some strong language. Also
issued on flexible disc as FD 17707.
Bestseller 1981.

Northlight, Lovelight   RC 11174
by Jacques Folch-Ribas
translated by Jeremy J. Leggatt
narrated by Diane Heles
1 cassette
Bittersweet story of Pierre and Marie,
two lonely orphans who share young
love and one idyllic summer of happiness in the wilderness of northeast
Canada. 1976.

**The French Lieutenant's Woman
RC 17851**
by John Fowles
narrated by Douglas Seale
3 cassettes
A mid-Victorian novel set in England
in the 1860s and 1870s, but with a
contemporary narrator. An educated
governess, betrayed by a French lieutenant, attracts a man who is engaged
to marry the rich, shallow daughter of
a merchant prince. 1969.

The Bleeding Heart   RC 15090
by Marilyn French
narrated by Yvonne Fair Tessler
3 cassettes
An account of an intense love affair
between two Americans living in England without their families. A writer-
feminist, "the original bleeding
heart," meets a businessman in a
compartment of the London-Oxford
train. Their attraction is mutual.
Strong language and explicit descriptions of sex. Also issued on flexible
disc as FD 15090. Bestseller. 1980.

To the Opera Ball   RC 10561
by Sarah Gainham
narrated by Patricia Beaudry
3 cassettes
Love story about Leona, the product
of wealth and privilege, and Rolf, a
war orphan of unknown parentage,
who meet at the Vienna Opera Ball
and run away together. Leona's out-
raged father tries to end the affair.
1975.

Love and Glory   RC 18806
by Patricia Hagan
narrated by Mitzi Friedlander
3 cassettes
After the tribulations of the Civil
War, the passionate romance between
Travis Coltrane and Kitty Wright cul-
minates in marriage and a peaceful
life on their North Carolina farm.
However, restlessness lures Travis
away on a long trip, and when he
returns, he finds that his bride has

disappeared. Strong language and explicit descriptions of sex. 1982.

The Winds of Summer   RC 10564
by Arlene Hale
narrated by Patricia Beaudry
2 cassettes
Sociology teacher Fleur Lansing learns that her sister has become seriously involved with an older man known for his unsavory reputation. She returns home to her family in Gold Rush City, a thriving Wild West tourist attraction. 1976.

Shakespeare Girl   RC 20194
by Mollie Hardwick
narrated by Richard Clarke
2 cassettes
In the early 1900s, Miranda Heriot, who is brought up by fanatically moralistic grandparents, leaves home to join a theater troupe at Stratford-on-Avon. There she falls for and is rejected by a dashing actor, but recovers when journalist Andrew Craigie claims her heart. 1983.

Castle of Eagles   RC 7902
by Constance Heaven
narrated by Patricia Beaudry
3 cassettes
In 1847, Lisa Heron, an outstanding young pianist, leads a busy, exciting life in Vienna. She is pursued by the headstrong Rudi, but soon finds herself in love with his aristocratic uncle, Julian. 1974.

This Is the House   RC 10436
by Deborah Hill
narrated by Patricia Beaudry
4 cassettes
Historical tale, set in New England after the American Revolution, about Molly Deems, who was reared as a servant in the home of a Quaker woman. After she is seduced by Isaac Warden, Molly marries Elijah Merrick, a respectable, rising young seaman. Some strong language and some explicit descriptions of sex. 1975.

The Autumn Rose   RC 12819
by Fiona Hill
narrated by Elizabeth Swain
2 cassettes
Outspoken, sparkling, twenty-three-year-old Lady Caro Wythe is sent to Georgian London to marry, though she has no desire to. Her marriage consultant urges her to become an eccentric by smoking cigars and wearing mannish attire. 1978.

The Love Child   RC 11924
by Fiona Hill
narrated by Gerry Kasarda
1 cassette
Eighteenth-century tale about outspoken Lotta Chilton of mysterious origins who hires out as companion to the haughty old Duchess of Karr. Lotta wins the heart of the young heir despite objections to the marriage. 1977.

By Way of the Silverthorns   RC 18349
by Grace Livingston Hill
narrated by Dale Carter
2 cassettes
With the help of a sophisticated young man, a vivacious girl from the country adjusts to the complexities of modern living in this old-fashioned novel. 1941.

Time of the Singing of Birds   RC 7843
by Grace Livingston Hill
narrated by Dorothy Eckel
3 cassettes
A proud young schoolteacher contends with a glamorous, scheming woman for the love of a war-scarred hero. 1970.

**Red Sky at Night, Lovers' Delight?
RC 12555**
by Jane Aiken Hodge
narrated by Jill Tanner
2 cassettes
In early nineteenth-century England, fiery Kate and her mother lose their house and land to an American cousin. When they take positions as governess and housekeeper in rakish Lord Hawth's home, Kate is swept up in intrigue, adventure, and romance. 1977.

The Demon Lover   RC 18819
by Victoria Holt
narrated by Mitzi Friedlander
3 cassettes
Relates the adventures of young artist Kate Collison in England and France during the mid-1800s. Kate takes over the commissions of her father, a famed miniaturist, when his sight fails. She meets a French baron and initially despises him for his arrogance, but she later comes to love him. 1982.

The Devil on Horseback   RC 11122
by Victoria Holt
narrated by Etain O'Malley
3 cassettes
During the French Revolution, Wilhelmina Maddox, spirited daughter of an English schoolmistress, falls in love with a French count. Both face death when family turmoil erupts. Also issued on flexible disc as FD 11122. 1977.

Close Relations   RC 16567
by Susan Isaacs
narrated by Mitzi Friedlander
3 cassettes
Marcia Green is a witty Jewish political speechwriter who enjoys a passionate but unpromising live-in relationship with a dashing Irish co-worker. Marcia's life is uncomplicated until she falls in love with the answer to her family's fervent prayers—a rich, handsome, well-educated Jewish lawyer. Some strong language and some explicit descriptions of sex. 1980.

A Marriage of Convenience   RC 13834
by Tim Jeal
narrated by Yvonne Fair Tessler
3 cassettes
A Victorian tale involves two brothers

in love with the actress Theresa, a widow whose wit and free spirit charms them both. Wealthy lawyer Esmond, the discarded illegitimate son of a peer, rises to the top of his profession. His handsome, debt-ridden brother Clinton, a cavalry officer, inherits the title and the ancestral home. Whom will Theresa choose? Some strong language. Also issued on flexible disc as FD 13834. 1979.

Love, Etc.   RC 13989
by Bel Kaufman
narrated by Yvonne Fair Tessler
3 cassettes
Still recovering from the trauma of a recent divorce, a middle-aged woman works toward wholeness and fulfillment in her life. After she enters into an intensely romantic, star-crossed, love affair with an enigmatic stranger, she discovers he is a charlatan. Some strong language. Also issued on flexible disc as FD 13989. 1979.

Beauty and Sadness   RC 9221
by Yasunari Kawabata
translated by Howard Hibbett
narrated by Harold Scott
2 cassettes
A lyrical, erotic, love story and the last novel written before Kawabata's death. Oki Toshio, an aging novelist, longs to see his mistress, whom he abandoned twenty-four years before. Now a painter, Otoko lives with a lesbian protégée who acts to avenge her and to destroy Oki. 1975.

The Far Pavilions   RC 12947
by M. M. Kaye
narrated by Jill Ferris
9 cassettes in two containers
Panoramic novel of adventure and romance set in nineteenth-century British India. Focuses on Ash, an English officer raised as a Hindu at the foot of the Himalayas—the "Far Pavilions." His love for a beautiful Eurasian princess transcends separation, adversity, and cultural prejudice. Also issued on flexible disc as FD 12947. 1978.

Circle of Love   RC 16821
by Syrell Rogovin Leahy
narrated by Michael McCullough
2 cassettes
The love story of Anna, a German Jew who was sent to live in France with a protective aunt during World War II, and Anton, a Polish survivor of a Nazi concentration camp. Searching for her parents after the war, Anna meets Anton when they both stumble upon the same abandoned farmhouse. The memorable three days they spend there comforting and loving each other haunt Anna even after she finds a comfortable life in the United States and a man who loves her. 1980.

The Vermilion Gate: A Novel of a Far Land   RC 16744
by Yutang Lin
narrated by Suzanne Toren
3 cassettes
Set in China in the 1930s. Tells of the

courtship of Li Fei, a roving correspondent, and Jo-An Tu, daughter of a liberal-minded scholar. Realizing that she is pregnant before marriage and that this would be an unpardonable offense against both families, Jo-An follows Li Fei into exile. 1953.

Hot Type   RC 18431
by Marjorie Lipsyte
narrated by Laura Giannarelli
2 cassettes
Twenty-six-year-old Arlyn Crane is a secretary in New York City at a renowned daily, the *Paper*. It is 1960 and Arlyn hungers for a career as a reporter as well as for a husband and children in a suburb. Then she falls in love with married Bill Hallam, hotshot newsman and male chauvinist. Strong language and some explicit descriptions of sex. 1980.

I Take This Man   RC 20190
by Emilie Loring
narrated by Mimi Bederman
2 cassettes
When twenty-three-year-old Penelope marries Donald Garth, millionaire president of the Garth airplane plant, she becomes mistress of Uplands, a palatial estate. But Penny knows from the very first day of her marriage that there is a secret barrier between herself and her husband, and that she is not to blame. 1958.

A Key to Many Doors   RC 17946
by Emilie Loring
narrated by Bets Thompson
2 cassettes
Almost resigned to her life as a spinster nurse, Nancy impulsively proposes to diplomat artist Peter Gerad. Trapped in a "marriage of convenience," she realizes that she is falling in love with him. 1967.

Friends and Lovers   RC 12289
by Helen MacInnes
narrated by Janet Marchmont
3 cassettes
David Botsworth, a poor Oxford scholar on a pilgrimage to a Scottish island, falls in love at first sight with a woman from a conventional family. David must overcome the young woman's mother's objections before the romance can succeed. 1947.

The Fen Tiger   RC 15331
by Catherine Marchant
narrated by Patricia Beaudry
2 cassettes
Though Rosamund Morley is two years younger than her beautiful sister Jennifer, it is Rosamund who had always looked after her sister and their alcoholic father in the lonely millhouse in the Fens where they live. Searching for help during one of her father's drinking bouts, she runs into Michael, a hostile neighbor guarding a dark secret. Their relationship turns into love. 1963.

Reap the Savage Wind   RC 18679
by Ellen Tanner Marsh
narrated by Dale Carter
3 cassettes
An eighteenth-century English beauty's efforts to restore her family's fortune and find true love. Some descriptions of sex. Bestseller. 1982.

Embers of Dawn   RC 17736
by Patricia Matthews
narrated by Jill Ferris
2 cassettes
A determined Southern woman seeks love and money in the fiery aftermath of the Civil War. She finds herself torn between two men, one who offers wisdom and tenderness and another who introduces her to passion. Some strong language and some explicit descriptions of sex. Also issued on flexible disc as FD 17736. 1982.

Flames of Glory   RC 19936
by Patricia Matthews
narrated by Mitzi Friedlander
3 cassettes
The Spanish-American War looses three thousand soldiers on sultry Tampa, home of young Jessica Manning. Beautiful Jessica becomes a war prize herself in a battle between one man's selfish greed and another's blazing love. Explicit descriptions of sex. 1983.

Love's Wildest Promise   RC 12211
by Patricia Matthews
narrated by Michael McCullough
2 cassettes
Kidnapped and sold into white slavery, Sarah Moody depends upon ship captain Jeb Hawkins to rescue her. No sooner does he perceive Sarah's plight than he, too, becomes a victim and both are stranded in the wilderness of the Louisiana Territory. Some strong language. 1977.

Tides of Love   RC 17303
by Patricia Matthews
narrated by Jill Ferris
2 cassettes
In New England during the era of the great sailing ships, lovely Marianna is caught between her love for gentle Phillip and her passion for a forceful sea captain. Some strong language and some explicit descriptions of sex. Also issued on flexible disc as FD 17303. Bestseller. 1981.

Moonstruck Madness   RC 18808
by Laurie McBain
narrated by Madelyn Buzzard
3 cassettes
A tale of the beautiful Lady Sabrina Verrick and the dashing Lucien, Duke of Camareigh, whose first bloody encounter grows into a turbulent, fiery romance. Some descriptions of sex. 1977.

Tears of Gold   RC 14416
by Laurie McBain
narrated by Michael Clarke-Laurence
4 cassettes
Mara O'Flynn, fiery Irish temptress
and consummate actress, agrees to a
daring impersonation of another
woman that fools everyone except one
man—Nicholas de Montaigne Chan-
tale, a wealthy Creole whose dreams
are haunted by Mara's beauty.
Though he is sworn to kill her, she
is the love he would even die for.
Explicit descriptions of sex. 1979.

The Thorn Birds   RC 10497
by Colleen McCullough
narrated by Bob Askey
5 cassettes
Saga of the Cleary family set in a vast
Australian sheep station. Central figures are beautiful Meggie and the one
man she truly loves—the handsome
priest Ralph de Bricassart. Some
strong language and some explicit
descriptions of sex. Also issued on
flexible disc as FD 10497. 1977.

**Stealing Heaven: The Love Story of
Heloise and Abelard   RC 16182**
by Marion Meade
narrated by Patricia Beaudry
3 cassettes
Recreates the tragic story of the
celebrated twelfth-century lovers.
Heloise's uncle hires the philosopher
Abelard as the beautiful girl's tutor,
and inflicts a cruel punishment when
he discovers they are in love. Separated forever, Heloise enters a convent and Abelard becomes a monk.
The sometimes-passionate, elegant exchange of letters chronicles their past
and present relationship. Some strong
language and some explicit descriptions of sex. 1979.

Patriot's Dream   RC 11092
by Barbara Michaels
narrated by Myra Stennett
4 cassettes
When young Janice Wilde spends
the summer with her elderly aunt
and uncle in a restored house in
Williamsburg, she begins to dream of
Jonathan, who lived two hundred
years before. Her love for him is
stronger than her interest in two
young men who are courting her.
1976.

Captive Innocence   RC 17635
by Fern Michaels
narrated by Mitzi Friedlander
3 cassettes
A sheltered New England beauty and
a passionate Latin planter collide time
and again as owners of neighboring
plantations in tropical Brazil. As lovers, they surrender to a frenzy of desire that far exceeds their lustiest
fantasies. Some strong language and
explicit descriptions of sex. 1981.

The Doctor's Wife   RC 9756
by Brian Moore
narrated by Flo Gibson
2 cassettes
When her husband cannot accompany
her to France for what is intended to

be a second honeymoon, thirty-seven-year-old Sheila from Ulster meets and falls passionately in love with a much younger American. She must choose between her lover and her successful husband. Strong language and explicit descriptions of sex. 1976.

So Love Returns   RC 10514
by Robert Nathan
narrated by John Polk
1 cassette
A struggling young writer is left with the responsibility of raising his small daughter and son after the untimely death of his beloved wife. When a strange young woman saves his son from the sea, he falls in love with her. 1973.

The Braganza Pursuit   RC 10771
by Sarah Neilan
narrated by Azaleigh Maginnis
2 cassettes
Nineteen-year-old Adelaide Smith, who inherited her Irish mother's flaming red hair and romantic temper, is left without family or fortune when her father dies. Taking a job as a governess in the house of the Portuguese ambassador to London, she experiences danger and romance. 1976.

The Sterile Cuckoo   RC 18847
by John Nichols
narrated by Christopher Hurt
1 cassette
A rapturous, crazy, love affair between an effervescent heroine and a fun loving fraternity man who first

meet in a bus station. Some strong language. 1965.

Maria Canossa   RC 18548
by Sandra Paretti
translated by Ruth Hein
narrated by Patricia Beaudry
2 cassettes
In 1943, Maria Canossa, an Italian woman, leaves Hilter's Berlin and a loveless marriage to return to her native Rome. Amid the chaos and intrigue of a desperate city under German occupation, she falls in love for the first time with the mysterious Marco Varelli. 1981.

Amanda/Miranda   RC 15088
by Richard Peck
narrated by Jill Ferris
4 cassettes
Story set in the Edwardian period of 1911 moves among the Isle of Wight, London, and New York. It features two women: the wily, beautiful daughter of Lady Eleanor and Sir Timothy Whitwell, who was born to command, and her personal maid and look-alike, hard-working Miranda. Mistress and maid become locked in love and intrigue over chauffeur John Thorne. Some explicit descriptions of sex. Also issued on flexible disc as FD 15088. 1980.

Sleeping Tiger   RC 10511
by Rosamunde Pilcher
narrated by Amanda Hale-Royce
1 cassette
A quiet, sensible woman is ready to marry a quiet, sensible man until a

face from her past appears on a book jacket. Suddenly she departs for a Spanish island to search for a man thought to be dead for years and becomes entangled in the most impossible love affair of her life. 1967.

Wild Mountain Thyme   RC 13814
by Rosamunde Pilcher
narrated by Diane Eilenberg
2 cassettes
Victoria Bradshaw considers herself in love with a successful but caddish playwright who pops in and out of her life. When he reappears with a two-year-old son in tow, Victoria consents to a vacation in the Scottish highlands with them. Also issued on flexible disc as FD 13814. 1978.

A Long and Happy Life   RC 14827
by Reynolds Price
narrated by Eugenia Rawls
1 cassette
Rosacoke Mustian is in love with Wesley Beaver, a young man just out of the Navy and more interested in loose women and motorcycles than in her. 1961.

Found, Lost, Found   RC 14460
by J. B. Priestley
narrated by Richard Braun
1 cassette
A disillusioned, gin-drinking civil servant and a divorced, liberated sociologist are attracted to each other. She declares she will disappear into the English countryside and he never

will see her again unless he remains sober. 1976.

Live and Remember   RC 12070
by Valentin Rasputin
translated by Antonina W. Bouis
narrated by Steve Grad
2 cassettes
Set in wartime Siberia at the peasant hamlet of Atamanovka. Relates the tender and tragic love story of Andrei and Nastyona, who are separated by the German invasion during World War II. Repeatedly wounded and returned to the front, Andrei finally deserts, depending upon his wife to protect him. Some explicit descriptions of sex. 1978.

Summer of '42   RC 16418
by Herman Raucher
narrated by Dennis Bateman
2 cassettes
A middle-aged man returns to Packett Island off the New England coast and summons up memories of the summer of 1942 when he and his two buddies were fifteen. Preoccupied with sex, the three boys brooded, talked, read about it, and tried to turn theory into practice. Strong language. 1971.

**There Should Have Been Castles
RC 12692**
by Herman Raucher
narrated by Richard Braun and
Mitzi Friedlander
5 cassettes
A young man, Ben, becomes a successful TV playwright and a maverick Hollywood screenwriter. Ginnie, a

dancer, makes it big in New York. Their rapturous sex "castle" falls apart when Ginnie finds Ben cavorting with her mother. Strong language and explicit descriptions of sex. 1978.

Lost Ecstasy   RC 14732
by Mary Roberts Rinehart
narrated by Esther Benson
2 cassettes
Kay Dowling does not expect romance when she and her wealthy family visit her grandfather's ranch. It is unthinkable that she could ever be attracted to someone like cowboy Tom McNair, but there is no way to escape the dangerous game of love they begin. 1927.

Praise the Human Season   RC 11372
by Don Robertson
narrated by Ken Meeker
4 cassettes
Howard and Anne Amberson, in their seventies, set out on an auto trip to find the meaning of life. They discover that nothing is more important than their deep love for one another. 1974.

Dark Fires   RC 12232
by Rosemary Rogers
narrated by Suzanne Toren
4 cassettes
The turbulent but passionate marriage of Ginny and Steve Morgan is tried by events and desires that propel them across oceans and continents from old Mexico to Czarist Russia. Some strong language and some ex-

plicit descriptions of sex. Second part of a series. Followed by *Lost Love, Last Love (RC 16393)*. 1975.

Lost Love, Last Love   RC 16393
by Rosemary Rogers
narrated by Nancy Campbell
3 cassettes
Virginia and Steve, now married, are caught up in the turbulent events of the 1870s. Fate and time separate them as they set out on separate journeys from New Orleans to revolutionary Cuba to Mexico and to Europe. Some explicit descriptions of sex and some strong language. Third part of a series. Sequel to *Dark Fires (RC 12232)*. Bestseller. 1980.

Love Play   RC 17332
by Rosemary Rogers
narrated by Yvonne Fair Tessler
3 cassettes
Sara agrees to masquerade as her actress sister to cover the sister's elopement. The elaborate ruse backfires when a tempestuous romance develops between Sara, still posing as her sister, and the arrogant Italian duke who is the obstacle to her sister's marriage. Some strong language and descriptions of sex. Also issued on flexible disc as FD 17332. Bestseller. 1981.

Surrender to Love   RC 18619
by Rosemary Rogers
narrated by Becky Parker
4 cassettes
At her debutante ball, Alexa Howard,

the young daughter of a rich plantation owner, meets her cynical and arrogant cousin with whom she develops a passionate love-hate relationship. Some strong language and descriptions of sex. 1982.

Sweet Savage Love   RC 9236
by Rosemary Rogers
narrated by Linda Atwill
8 cassettes in two containers
A Paris-educated senator's daughter experiences high adventures and many love affairs in post-Civil War New Orleans, the West, and Mexico during the reign of Maximilian. Explicit descriptions of sex. First part of a series. Followed by *Dark Fires (RC 12232)*. 1974.

Mary Dove   RC 7898
by Jane Gilmore Rushing
narrated by Patricia Beaudry
3 cassettes
Alone in a remote part of Texas after the Civil War, Mary wounds a stranger who approaches her. While nursing him back to health, she falls in love with him. 1974.

Another I, Another You: A Love Story for the Once-Married   RC 15435
by Richard Schickel
narrated by George Guidall
2 cassettes
Two newly divorced people—he, an independent film maker; she, the wife of his best friend—discover that neither of them is the ogre that their spouses had claimed. Some strong

language and some explicit descriptions of sex. 1978.

Desiree   RC 10308
by Annemarie Selinko
narrated by Gerry Kasarda
4 cassettes
Relates in diary form how a charming silk merchant's daughter, once engaged to Napoleon, finds a new love and marries his general, Jean-Baptiste Bernadotte, who later becomes King of Sweden. 1953.

Hearth and the Eagle   RC 10558
by Anya Seton
narrated by Flo Gibson
3 cassettes
Relates the story of a two-hundred-year-old inn in the rocky New England seacoast town of Marblehead, Massachusetts, during the Civil War, and the lives and loves of red-haired Hesper Honeywood. 1976.

Rash, Reckless Love   RC 18394
by Valerie Sherwood
narrated by Noah Siegel
4 cassettes
Raised by foster parents as a Bermuda belle, proud, passionate Georgianna falls in and out of fortune until the man of her dreams sweeps her away. He also brings her the incredible story of her true identity and rightful inheritance. Followed by *Wild, Willful Love (RC 18681)*. Explicit descriptions of sex. 1982.

Wild, Willful Love   RC 18681
by Valerie Sherwood
narrated by Yvonne Fair Tessler
3 cassettes
When willful Imogene discovers her dashing buccaneer in another woman's arms, she returns to her girlhood home, where she is convicted of murder. Even as she faces certain death, though, Imogene knows that her Caribbean lord will come to the rescue. Sequel to *Rash, Reckless Love (RC 18394)*. Some strong language and some descriptions of sex. Also issued on flexible disc as FD 18681. Bestseller. 1982.

The Far Country   RC 8558
by Nevil Shute
narrated by Gillian Watson
4 cassettes
A London doctor's daughter on a visit to cousins to Australia meets a Czech surgeon. The two fall in love, and when Jennifer has to return to London, Carl decides to complete his studies there. 1952.

The Slave   RC 12441
by Isaac Bashevis Singer
translated from the Yiddish by the author and Cecil Hemley
narrated by George Guidall
2 cassettes
In seventeenth-century Poland, an intellectual and pious young Jew is driven from his native town by a cossack raid and becomes the slave of a Polish peasant. He loves, and is loved by, the peasant's daughter, but the

law forbids their marriage on pain of death. 1962.

Skye O'Malley   RC 18031
by Bertrice Small
narrated by Becky Parker
4 cassettes
The adventures of an Irish beauty in Algeria and Elizabethan England. Strong language and explicit descriptions of sex. 1980.

Unconquered   RC 17708
by Bertrice Small
narrated by Yvonne Fair Tessler
4 cassettes
Forced to marry an English cousin to keep her home, strong-willed Miranda Dunham grows to love her husband passionately. Traveling alone to Russia to find him when he is long overdue from a secret diplomatic mission, she is kidnapped by a Siberian slave breeder as the perfect match for his prize stud. Yet her spirit remains unbroken as her heart longs for only one man. Some strong language and explicit descriptions of sex. Also issued on flexible disc as FD 17708. 1982.

Changes   RC 19235
by Danielle Steel
narrated by Yvonne Fair Tessler
3 cassettes
Melanie Adams seems to have it all: success as a TV documentary producer, twin teenage daughters, and a glamorous life that's perfect for a single mother. But Peter Hallam, a

More Romances Cassettes

world-famous heart surgeon and wid-ower with three children, makes her realize she doesn't yet have every-thing she wants. Some strong lan-guage and some descriptions of sex. Also issued on flexible disc as FD 19235. Bestseller. 1983.

Crossings   RC 18668
by Danielle Steel
narrated by Ann Hodapp
3 cassettes
Aboard a luxury liner on the eve of World War II, the French ambassador to the United States and his American wife Liane meet wealthy Nick and Hillary Burnham. The spark between Nick and Liane is instantaneous. Not until a second fateful crossing, though, do they face the power and the hopelessness of their passion. Some strong language. 1982.

Palomino   RC 17343
by Danielle Steel
narrated by Jill Ferris
2 cassettes
A New York advertising executive flees to a California dude ranch after being ditched by her husband, a na-tionally known TV anchorman. On the range, Samantha does more than just forget; she falls madly in love with a rugged cowboy who promises her nothing but the irresistible passion of the moment. Some strong language and some explicit descriptions of sex. Also issued on flexible disc as FD 17343. Bestseller 1981.

A Perfect Stranger   RC 17723
by Danielle Steel
narrated by Yvonne Fair Tessler
2 cassettes
Raphaella loves her aging husband dearly and grieves that a stroke has incapacitated him. Almost against her will, she falls in love with Alex, a vi-rile young California attorney. But their love is tinged with Raphaella's guilt that her life is just beginning as her husband's is ending. Some strong language and some descriptions of sex. Also issued on flexible disc as FD 17723. Bestseller. 1981.

Remembrance   RC 17324
by Danielle Steel
narrated by Jill Ferris
3 cassettes
An impoverished Italian-born princess marries a wealthy army officer after World War II. She endures a hateful mother-in-law until the Korean Con-flict makes her a widow. Serena be-comes a successful fashion model and marries again, with tragic conse-quences. Also issued on flexible disc as FD 17324. Bestseller. 1981.

The Ring   RC 15810
by Danielle Steel
narrated by Pam Ward
2 cassettes
Supposedly based on an actual inci-dent in the author's own family. Tells of a rich German woman, Kassandra von Gotthard, who falls in love with a Jewish writer, Dolff Stern. Their hap-piness is short-lived, for the Nazis

92

soon murder Stern, causing Kassandra to take her own life. Some strong language. Also issued on flexible disc as FD 15810. 1980.

To Love Again   RC 18106
by Danielle Steel
narrated by Ann Hodapp
2 cassettes
Isabella and Amadeo, the darlings of international society, rule the House of San Gregorio, the most respected name in Rome couture. Though their lives are rich and full, nothing outshines their enduring love for one another. One day Amadeo is kidnapped and brutally murdered and Isabella doubts she will ever love again. Some strong language. Bestseller 1980.

The Dresden Finch   RC 11100
by Jessica Stirling
narrated by Mitzi Friedlander
2 cassettes
A lusty heroine survives tragedy, danger, and the wiles of a domineering governess. Some strong language and some explicit descriptions of sex. 1976.

**The President's Lady: A Novel about Rachel and Andrew Jackson
RC 9463**
by Irving Stone
narrated by Dale Carter
3 cassettes
A fictionalized biography about Rachel, who married Andrew Jackson in spite of some doubts about the legality of her divorce. A love story set against the background of westward expansion in America and the War of 1812. 1959.

Love among the Ruins   RC 7738
by Angela Thirkell
narrated by Patricia Beaudry
6 cassettes
Describes the romance between Susan Dean and Captain Belton. Also chronicles an English family's efforts to adapt to post-war conditions in the fictional county of Barsetshire. 1948.

Chase the Wind   RC 11534
by E. V. Thompson
narrated by Burt Blackwell
3 cassettes
Story about Josh Retallick, ambitious son and grandson of Cornish copper miners, and his childhood sweetheart, a reckless young beauty of the moors. A tragic misunderstanding drives each to a temporary marriage doomed to disaster. Some explicit descriptions of sex. 1977.

Parker's Island   RC 13837
by Joan Thompson
narrated by Diane Eilenberg
2 cassettes
In 1892 on Parker's Island off the coast of Massachusetts, eighteen-year-old Gwyn works for a summer as a chambermaid at the inn. There, she and Tom, a wealthy vacationing Bostonian, become lovers. After Tom's departure, Gwyn discovers she is pregnant and marries fifty-year-old Ethan, a family friend. 1979.

More Romances

The Flowering RC 17053
by Agnes Sligh Turnbull
narrated by Anne Mullen
2 cassettes
Hester Carr, a widow in her thirties, yearns for a way of life aside from devotion to her cocker spaniel and music. Then John Justin comes to the suburb of Westbrook to write a book. 1972.

Remember the End RC 11828
by Agnes Sligh Turnbull
narrated by George Backman
3 cassettes
A young Scottish immigrant comes to America in the 1890s and settles in Pennsylvania coal country. He fights his way to the top to become a coal baron, but almost loses his love in his drive for success. 1938.

Whistle and I'll Come to You
RC 20186
by Agnes Sligh Turnbull
narrated by Connie Lembcke
2 cassettes
An old-fashioned romance about a local girl and her handsome English beau. The townspeople distrust the young man after two wealthy old spinsters make him their heir. 1970.

The Very Best People RC 13840
by Elizabeth Villars
narrated by Jill Ferris
2 cassettes
Spunky Kathryn Owen from an Irish immigrant background and aristocratic Tyson fall in love, but the snobbery in his family keeps them apart for years. Also issued on flexible disc as FD 13840. 1979.

Ash RC 10571
by David Walker
narrated by Ken Meeker
2 cassettes
Recuperating from an illness in a log cabin in the beautiful Canadian woods, former fighter pilot Nigel Ash falls in love with his brother's wife Lorna. Some strong language. 1976.

Stranger from the North RC 12534
by Lucy Walker
narrated by Elizabeth Swain
2 cassettes
Life on a cattle station in the Australian Outback is rough, and since her father's death, Gerry has had to take over his work. Then a mysterious arrogant stranger rides in and takes over the management of the station. She dislikes his high-handed ways, but, in spite of herself, she seems to be letting him take over her heart. 1976.

The Quicksilver Pool RC 10430
by Phyllis A. Whitney
narrated by Ruth Stokesberry
3 cassettes
Begins with the loveless marriage of a wounded Union officer and the Southern girl who nurses him and eases the tragic and mysterious loss of his first wife. 1955.

The Adventuress   RC 15264
by Daoma Winston
narrated by Sheena Gordon
2 cassettes
On election night, 1896, in Annapolis, Maryland, a young widow stumbles upon a man sprawled across her front walk and takes him into her home. She learns that he is the newly elected state attorney general who has been drugged by a rival. The encounter sparks a romance that is the start of a new life for her. 1978.

Ashes in the Wind   RC 15764
by Kathleen E. Woodiwiss
narrated by Michael McCullough
4 cassettes
A Cajun carpetbagger spreads rumors that Alaina MacGaren is a traitor, and drives the resourceful seventeen-year-old orphan from her family's Virginia plantation to war-ravaged New Orleans. To preserve her anonymity, Alaina disguises herself and finds her fate entangled with that of a gentlemanly surgeon, Yankee Captain Cole Lattimer. Bestseller. 1979.

The Flame and the Flower   RC 11900
by Kathleen E. Woodiwiss
narrated by Wesley Llewellyn
3 cassettes
The passionate and often-violent romance of Heather Simmons and Captain Brandon Birmingham spans oceans and continents, from Heather's kidnapping at a squalid London wharf to the splendor of Brandon's Carolina plantation. Explicit descriptions of sex. Also issued on flexible disc as FD 11900. 1972.

A Rose in Winter   RC 18688
by Kathleen E. Woodiwiss
narrated by Yvonne Fair Tessler
4 cassettes
Erienne Flemming, daughter of the self-indulgent and debt-ridden mayor of a bleak English hamlet, has the misfortune to fall in love with a dashingly handsome Yankee. She suffers the added indignity of being sold by her father in marriage to her richest suitor, a hideously deformed nobleman who hides behind black leather mask, gloves, and cloak. Explicit descriptions of sex. Also issued on flexible disc as FD 18688. Bestseller. 1982.

Shanna   RC 10784
by Kathleen E. Woodiwiss
narrated by Jill Tanner
5 cassettes
In eighteenth-century London, Shanna must marry by her twenty-first birthday. Her father arranges a marriage of convenience with a condemned prisoner. Some explicit descriptions of sex. Also issued on flexible disc as FD 10784. 1977.

The Wolf and the Dove   RC 16595
by Kathleen E. Woodiwiss
narrated by Dion Chesse
4 cassettes
When the Normans conquer England in the eleventh century, Aislinn of Darkenwald, fiercely loyal to her own Saxon people, struggles against her

passion for Wulfgar, the Iron Wolf of Normandy. Can her love for Wulfgar drive out the memory of her father's murder, her mother's shame, and her own violation, all at the hands of the conquering Normans? Some descriptions of sex. 1974.

Braille

The Tamarind Seed   BR 2068
by Evelyn Anthony
2 volumes
After an unsuccessful love affair, a young widow escapes to Barbados and is attracted to a Russian intelligence agent. The romance causes suspicion in the Russian spy system and the agent's romance and career are threatened. Explicit descriptions of sex. 1971.

He Married a Doctor   BR 5101
by Faith Baldwin
2 volumes
Story of a doctor torn between the responsibilities of her medical career and the demands of her marriage. At first her husband seems to understand how important medicine is to her, but later he is tempted by the charms of another woman, who is prepared to devote all her time to him. 1944.

The Lonely Man   BR 5120
by Faith Baldwin
2 volumes
A young doctor with a busy practice in a small New England town mourns the death of his wife. But even a busy man gets lonely—and Frances Lawson, a beautiful, rich divorcée, has designs on him. 1964.

Thursday's Child   BR 3369
by Faith Baldwin
2 volumes
Set in a gracious small village in New England where Sara Foster comes to live with her aristocratic grandmother. Sara takes a job at a friend's bookshop, meets co-owner Sam Peters and Paul Stevens, a playboy, and finally decides to marry one of them. 1976.

Both Your Houses   BR 2342
by James Barlow
3 volumes
Set in Belfast. A twenty-year-old Birmingham slum boy, a private in the British army, falls in love with the daughter of an unemployed Catholic IRA member. 1971.

**George beneath a Paper Moon
BR 2889**
by Nina Bawden
2 volumes
A successful travel agent finally marries in his mid-thirties and discovers his heart may belong to the daughter of his close friends. 1974.

Marry Me! Marry Me!   BR 1339
by Claude Berri
translated by June P. Wilson and Walter B. Michaels
1 volume
A simple story of love and marriage.

A young Frenchman from a humble background is in love with the spoiled daughter of a Belgian diamond dealer. Shortly before marrying her, he meets another woman and also falls in love with her. 1969.

The Jungle   BR 1810
by Charity Blackstock
3 volumes
Stella, a divorcée just a shade over forty, travels to the African jungles with a tour group. In the jungle she gains understanding of her relationship with her lover and insight into the tangle of her own emotions. 1972.

Tickets   BR 5027
by Richard P. Brickner
3 volumes
During intermission at the Metropolitan Opera, a debonair bachelor meets an enchanting married woman. Believing that life is full of significant surprises and as melodramatic as opera, the bachelor attempts to orchestrate their subsequent affair as he imagines it should be written, but the lovers are soon playing out their romance for real. Some strong language and explicit descriptions of sex. 1981.

The Famished Land: A Novel of the Irish Potato Famine   BR 2105
by Elizabeth Byrd
3 volumes
Moira McFlaherty and her big family live happily in a small village, where she dreams of the day she will marry her childhood sweetheart. When the famine comes, her courage sustains the family. 1972.

The Famished Land: A Novel of the Irish Potato Famine   BR 2477
by Elizabeth Byrd
6 volumes (Jumbo braille)
Moira McFlaherty and her big family live happily in a small village, where she dreams of the day she will marry her childhood sweetheart. When the famine comes, her courage sustains the family. 1972.

Home for the Wedding   BR 3912
by Elizabeth Cadell
2 volumes
Stacey Marsh, who has been living in Paris, returns to her English hometown to marry. While awaiting the arrival of her French fiancé, Stacey renews her relationship with a former suitor. 1972.

The Marrying Kind   BR 4522
by Elizabeth Cadell
2 volumes
Neither Jess Seton, impulsive, impatient, and beseiged by men, nor her easy-going, old-fashioned sister Laura is the marrying type. Their happy, independent lives are jolted when their father gets himself into trouble in Paris, and the sisters seek to help him. 1980.

The Round Dozen   BR 3898
by Elizabeth Cadell
2 volumes
In London, a rich bachelor is tracking down a priceless family heirloom missing since 1702. His sleuthing leads him into the rural countryside where he meets the Cambridgeshire secretary who not only helps him find the missing antique, but end his search for the perfect woman. 1978.

The Sleeping Salamander   BR 2497
by Catherine Carfax
2 volumes
Jan falls in love with Alain while on vacation and accompanies him on a mysterious trip to the wild coast of Brittany. There, in a deserted house, they become involved with the jewels of Madame de Chateaubriand, mistress of King Francis the First, "The Salamander King." 1973.

The Lion Triumphant   BR 3972
by Philippa Carr
3 volumes
During the reign of Elizabeth I, dashing, devil-may-care, sea captain Jake Pennlyon sails into the life of headstrong Catherine. Theirs is a tempestuous, though seemingly cursed, romance. 1974.

The Love Child   BR 3986
by Philippa Carr
3 volumes
Set against the post-Reformation background of England. Priscilla Eversleigh, at fourteen, has an impassioned love affair with a man on the run from religious and political troubles. He is captured by the king's men and beheaded before Priscilla secretly bears his child. Some strong language. Second part of a series. Sequel to *The Miracle at St. Bruno's (BR 3911)*. 1978.

The Miracle at St. Bruno's   BR 3911
by Philippa Carr
4 volumes
Set during the sinister and uncertain times of Henry VIII's England, the tale is told by a young woman, daughter of a beheaded lawyer, who marries an appealing man of questionable birth. Tragedy looms as both the young man and a treasure vanish. First part of a series. Followed by *The Love Child (BR 3986)*. 1976.

The Adventurer   BR 3909
by Barbara Cartland
2 volumes
After a long career of breaking hearts, Frank—a dashing hero—is reunited with his true love during World War I. When he discovers that his beloved is a German spy, he must decide whether to betray his heart or his country. 1977.

**The Chieftain without a Heart
BR 4535**
by Barbara Cartland
2 volumes
When the Duke of Strathnarn reluctantly arrives from London to claim his inheritance as chieftain of clan

McNarn, he finds the neighboring clans feuding. The chieftain of the clan Kilcraig bargains for peace by insisting that the duke marry his daughter. 1978.

The Flame Is Love   BR 5560
by Barbara Cartland
2 volumes
Engaged against her will to an English duke, a rich, sheltered, American girl is delighted to find herself temporarily stranded in Paris without a chaperone. The unexpected freedom leads her into some of the most dissolute pleasure palaces in Europe and into love at first sight. 1975.

The Ghost Who Fell in Love   BR 4179
by Barbara Cartland
2 volumes
Set in 1822 during the Royal Race Week at Ascot. A young girl is hidden by her brother in the secret priest's room of the manor house now rented out to a dashing earl. Smitten by the handsome nobleman, she pretends she is a ghost and warns her beloved of the plots she overhears against him. 1978.

The Judgement of Love   BR 4313
by Barbara Cartland
2 volumes
A young heiress visits her guardian's English estate. There she is introduced to his three nephews in hopes she will marry one. 1978.

A King in Love   BR 5257
by Barbara Cartland
2 volumes
Audacious young Princess Zita is determined to meet a visiting king whom her parents hope to snare for their elder daughter. Zita disguises herself as a waitress in order to meet the king, reputed to be as disreputable as he is handsome, and their brief encounter changes the course of her life. 1982.

Love and the Loathsome Leopard
BR 4345
by Barbara Cartland
2 volumes
Lord Cheriton, beloved of Wivina, is actually the "Leopard," determined to destroy a band of smugglers and terrorists headed by a man who swears he will marry Wivina. 1977.

Love at the Helm   BR 4916
by Barbara Cartland, inspired and helped by Admiral of the Fleet, the Earl Mountbatten of Burma
1 volume
When Captain Horn is ordered to sail to Antigua to deal with American privateers who are attacking British merchant ships, part of his mission is to carry with him the future wife of the governor of Antigua. Horn dislikes having a woman on board in wartime, even more so when she is his cousin and the sister of a man he detests. Nevertheless he is attracted to her. 1981.

Love for Sale   BR 4821
by Barbara Cartland
2 volumes
When Udela Hayward's father dies, Lord Julius Westry offers her employment in London. Delighted at first, she soon realizes that the destination of the carriage sent to meet her is a brothel. She runs away into the arms of the Duke of Westry, the brother of the rakish lord. 1980.

Love in the Clouds   BR 4374
by Barbara Cartland
2 volumes
Chandra Wardell's father, a famous Sanskrit scholar, is commissioned by Lord Frome to accompany him to Nepal. When the eminent professor suffers a heart attack, Chandra, who has helped her father for many years, goes in his place. On her arrival she encounters the anger of woman-hating Frome, but their antipathy to each other lessens when they discover a sacred manuscript and become involved in danger. 1979.

Love Is Innocent   BR 5233
by Barbara Cartland
2 volumes
The Duke of Atherstone has deftly avoided the scores of marriage traps set for him by determined mothers, their debutante daughters, and even his own jaded mistress. His heart finally goes to a most unlikely and unreachable candidate, a young English girl on sale in the Algerian slave market. 1975.

This Time It's Love   BR 3897
by Barbara Cartland
2 volumes
Nothing could be further from Fenella's mind than romance when Major Rex Ransome appears at her door. Suddenly she is swept off her feet, but a flurry of gossip threatens her father and promises to hurt Rex. 1977.

The Silver Leopard   BR 3356
by Zoe Cass
2 volumes
Set in the Scottish highland moors and mists. Caroline Westwood, who leaves her London antique shop and returns to her family home upon the news of her mother's death, is caught in a net of romance and terror. 1976.

Blind Love   BR 2953
by Patrick Cauvin
translated by Elaine P. Halperin
2 volumes
A shy Parisian professor vacationing in the South of France meets Laura, a vivacious blind woman. Their encounter leads to madcap adventures, as well as conflicts that threaten to destroy their idyll. Explicit descriptions of sex. 1975.

A Change of Heart   BR 4029
by Laura Chapman
2 volumes
Demure Tina Mallard spends a few months at an exclusive island retreat chaperoning her precocious cousins. Amidst a whirl of dances, days on the

beach, and two beaus, Tina blossoms. 1976.

Darlin' Bill BR 5158
by Jerome Charyn
3 volumes
The adventures of Sally Ovenshine, a Galveston woman who, while traveling through the Old West with her husband, meets and falls in love with the legendary Wild Bill Hickok. 1980.

Tilly BR 4703
by Catherine Cookson
4 volumes
During the early reign of Queen Victoria, teenage orphan Tilly Trotter lives with her widowed grandmother, who dies after their place is set afire. Homeless Tilly is hired by mine owner Mark Sopwith to be nursemaid to his four rambunctious children, whom she is able to handle. Later she becomes Mark's housekeeper, and affection grows into love. Some strong language. First part of a three-book series. Followed by *Tilly Wed (BR 4839)*. 1980.

Tilly Alone BR 5046
by Catherine Cookson
3 volumes
Widowed Tilly Trotter, now in her fifties, returns to England with two children after Comanche Indians kill her husband on the Texas frontier. When Tilly sees her childhood sweetheart again after many years, she begins to regret a promise she made her beloved husband on his deathbed. Last

part of a three-book series. Sequel to *Tilly Wed (BR 4839)*. 1982.

Tilly Wed BR 4839
by Catherine Cookson
3 volumes
Continues the saga of love and adversity of the English beauty. Pregnant and with her lover dead, Tilly is spared further persecution from the Sopwith family and the villagers when Mark Sopwith marries her and sweeps her off to Texas. She manages to triumph over the rigors of frontier life, her husband's jealous uncle, and the threats of Indian attacks. Some strong language. Second part of a three-book series. Followed by *Tilly Alone (BR 5046)*. 1981.

The Gate of Eden BR 3132
by William Corlett
1 volume
Covers one year in the middle-class lives of a young man, a young woman, and a mysterious old bachelor who is a teacher. Some strong language. 1974.

The Hour Awaits BR 4617
by March Cost
2 volumes
Relates two visits to London by an Austrian princess. During six months of 1911, she has a secret love affair with an English don. In 1921, returning on a family mission, she tries to recapture the joys of that earlier visit. 1952.

Calder Born, Calder Bred   BR 5637
by Janet Dailey
4 volumes
Ty was born a Calder but bred a stranger to his legacy, the vast ranchlands that stretch to meet the Montana sky. He learns the ways of ranch life from young Jessy, who knows the land like her own heart and would give anything for the love of Ty Calder. But Ty worships glamorous Tara, the greedy daughter of a powerful Texas millionaire. Fourth part of a series. Sequel to *Stands a Calder Man (BR 5333)*. Some strong language and some explicit descriptions of sex. Bestseller. 1983.

Ride the Thunder   BR 4767
by Janet Dailey
3 volumes
A glamorous New York socialite on a hunting party out west meets a rugged stranger whose fiery touch sparks her passion. Their romantic idyll is shattered by a terrible secret that claims one life and threatens to destroy another. Some strong language. 1980.

Stands a Calder Man   BR 5333
by Janet Dailey
2 volumes
Webb Calder is used to fighting man and nature to get what he wants. When homesteaders flock to Montana to seize their share of the American dream and, incidentally, to cramp the Calders' style, Webb finds among them the only woman he has ever wanted. Third part of a series. Fol-

lowed by *Calder Born, Calder Bred (BR 5637)*. Bestseller. 1983.

This Calder Range   BR 5094
by Janet Dailey
4 volumes
Story of a determined young rancher and the beautiful but practical bride who rides beside him to the Montana range. Old grudges and debts follow the settlers into the new land as they breathe life into a dream of freedom and a promise of riches. First part of a series. Followed by *This Calder Sky (BR 5052)*. Some explicit descriptions of sex. Bestseller. 1982.

This Calder Sky   BR 5052
by Janet Dailey
4 volumes
The great Calder empire stretches across the Montana plains as far as the eye can see. Everyone knows a Calder's word is law, and that one day Chase Calder will take the reins of power and carry the name to new glories. But for handsome, arrogant Chase there is also beautiful, headstrong Maggie O'Rourke, who is determined to be free of harsh codes. Second part of a series. Followed by *Stands a Calder Man (BR 5333)*. Bestseller. 1981.

Georgina   BR 1794
by Clare Darcy
3 volumes
A young English lady who has been raised by her grandparents upsets them by refusing a proposal of mar-

riage offered by a respectable young man. She is sent to Ireland, where she falls in love with an Irish man of whom they thoroughly disapprove. 1971.

Mary Wakefield   BR 5045
by Mazo de la Roche
3 volumes
A young Englishwoman is hired by Ernest Whiteoak to be governess to Philip's motherless children. When Philip falls in love with her, his mother does all she can to prevent the marriage. Third part of a sixteen-book series. Sequel to *Morning at Jalna (BR 4575)*. Followed by *Young Renny (BR 5032)*. 1973.

Renny's Daughter   BR 2806
by Mazo de la Roche
4 volumes
Renny's daughter travels to Ireland and becomes involved in a frustrating romance. Fourteenth part of a sixteen-book series. Sequel to *Return to Jalna (BR 5143)*. Followed by *Variable Winds at Jalna (BR 5038)*. 1951.

Wakefield's Course   BR 5037
by Mazo de la Roche
3 volumes
The continuing saga of the Whiteoak family in Canada from the spring of 1939 to the fall of 1940. Focuses on Wakefield, a successful actor, and his bittersweet love affair. Twelfth part of a sixteen book series. Sequel to *Whiteoak Harvest (BR 5036)*. Fol-

lowed by *Return to Jalna (BR 5143)*. 1973.

The Realms of Gold   BR 2880
by Margaret Drabble
5 volumes
A divorced mother of four, Frances Wingate is a famous archaeologist in love with a distinguished scholar, who is married. Some strong language. 1975.

Frenchman's Creek   BR 3329
by Daphne du Maurier
2 volumes
Set in England during the Restoration period. The central figures are the lovely Lady Dona, her slow-witted husband, and a dashing French pirate who captures the lady's love, but not the lady. 1942.

The Millionaire's Daughter   BR 2604
by Dorothy Eden
3 volumes
Cristabel Spencer, the young daughter of a rich American, is sent to London, where she captivates a young aristocrat, the Earl of Monkshood. When their marriage fails, she turns to a gifted artist. 1974.

Margaret Normanby   BR 5554
by Josephine Edgar
4 volumes
In Victorian England, spirited Margaret Normanby is born into a titled but dissipated family. Determined to "make money rather than spend it," she uses her talent for business to go

into trade, much to the shock of her family. As a convenience, she marries her business partner, a homosexual, although her heart belongs to another man. Some descriptions of sex. 1983.

Fortune's Wheel   BR 4099
by Rhoda Edwards
3 volumes
Plantagenet England and the Wars of the Roses provide the panoramic backdrop for this version of the marriage of Richard of Gloucester and Anne, daughter of the Earl of Warwick. Their deep love overcomes the awesome royal political forces pitted against them. 1979.

Willow Cabin   BR 2511
by Mary K. Fiandt
2 volumes
Katie Fuller, a thirty-four-year-old nurse, faces the impending end of a twelve-year love affair with Ben Feldman, a successful doctor who cares for the lonely and elderly. 1974.

Chelsea   BR 4730
by Nancy Fitzgerald
2 volumes
A Victorian novel about the romance of a portrait painter and his model, an orphaned nursemaid. The comedy and fluttery complications are provided by a failing cast-iron furniture business named Fluster and Muddle and characters that include Veracity Flutterby and a titled lady and her marriageable daughter. 1979.

The Playhouse   BR 4698
by Elaine Ford
2 volumes
Nurse Maureen Mullen becomes pregnant by a terminal cancer patient, a prominent politico, and quickly marries a boy she has known since childhood. Unexpressed grief for the father of her child leaves her indifferent to her husband, who feels the estrangement much more keenly than Maureen realizes. Some strong language. 1980.

Travels with a Duchess   BR 730
by Menna Gallie
2 volumes
Two married women, one Welsh and the other Irish, meet while vacationing in Yugoslavia, and have some wild adventures, including one woman's affair with two American bachelors. 1968.

Conventional Wisdom   BR 2351
by John Bart Gerald
1 volume
Disillusionment sets in immediately after the wedding of Will and his college bride. Then Will sacrifices his marriage for a more intense love. 1972.

The Leavetaking   BR 4541
by Anna Gilbert
2 volumes
Tale of love and loss in late Victorian England focuses on the search for young Lydia Lorne, cousin of Isobel Penrose. Lydia loves Isobel's widowed

father, but disappears when she finds her love tainted. 1980.

A Time for Us BR 2339
by Arlene Hale
2 volumes
Corliss never stops believing in or loving the man who had first captivated her as a girl. As a brash young man, he promised that there would be a time for their love. 1972.

The Masqueraders BR 3482
by Georgette Heyer
3 volumes
Temporarily abandoned by their reckless father, Prudence and her brother Robin Lacey masquerade as the opposite sex to avoid capture by their political enemies. This creates some dangerous entanglements when Prue falls in love with Sir Anthony and Robin is smitten by a lovely heiress. 1967.

The Talisman Ring BR 1283
by Georgette Heyer
7 volumes
An unsolved murder mystery, a band of smugglers, and a lost ring are inextricably mixed with the love affairs of a young French girl and her cousins in eighteenth-century England. 1966.

Harold and Maude BR 1691
by Colin Higgins
1 volume
The romance blossoms in this black comedy when nineteen-year-old Harold meets eighty-year-old Maude at a funeral. Harold is a young man with problems who stages fake suicides to terrify his mother, while Maude is an eccentric in love with life and living. 1971.

Amorelle BR 3754
by Grace Livingston Hill
2 volumes
Although engaged, Amorelle does not find true love until she is attracted to a young man. Her happiness soon fades, however, when she learns another woman has already claimed her beloved's heart. 1934.

By Way of the Silverthorns BR 4548
by Grace Livingston Hill
2 volumes
With the help of a sophisticated young man, a vivacious girl from the country adjusts to the complexities of modern living in this old-fashioned novel. 1941.

Madsong BR 1475
by Serena Sue Hilsinger
2 volumes
Follows a woman through a crucial year in her life in which she has a love affair and gets married. During the year she has frequent dialogues with an imaginary friend. 1970.

Stepping Out BR 4648
by Rolaine Hochstein
2 volumes
A story of two star-crossed lovers, she an almost-forty Jewish housewife who needs to be cherished, he a past-fifty

WASP lawyer who thinks he is over the hill. Some strong language and some explicit descriptions of sex. 1977.

The Lost Garden   BR 5297
by Jane Aiken Hodge
3 volumes
Set amid the glitter and scandal of early nineteenth-century London. Adopted at birth by a country vicar and his kind wife, Caroline is one day whisked away to live with a callous duke and his peculiar family at their Norfolk mansion. Stunned to learn the truth of her parentage, Caroline contracts a disastrous marriage and unwittingly involves herself in a deadly tangle of treason, torture, and murder. 1982.

The Demon Lover   BR 5255
by Victoria Holt
3 volumes
Relates the adventures of young artist Kate Collison in England and France during the mid-1800s. Kate takes over the commissions of her father, a famed miniaturist, when his sight fails. She meets a French baron and, initially, despises him for his arrogance, but she later comes to love him. 1982.

The Devil on Horseback   BR 3760
by Victoria Holt
3 volumes
During the French revolution, Wilhelmina Maddox, spirited daughter of an English schoolmistress, falls in love

with a French count. Both face death when family turmoil erupts. 1977.

The Jade Pagoda   BR 5144
by Betty Hale Hyatt
2 volumes
During the nineteenth century, Tawny Butler, an unmarried English gentlewoman recovering from an illicit affair, arrives in exotic Kashmir in search of her brother, a government agent in her majesty's secret service. She encounters many dangers and discovers her love for Lord Gordon Harding, who hires her to accompany his headstrong sister through Nepal and Tibet. 1980.

How Do I Love Thee   BR 3236
by Lucille Iremonger
4 volumes
Fictional account of the passionate love affair and happy marriage of English poets Elizabeth and Robert Browning. 1976.

Close Relations   BR 4753
by Susan Isaacs
3 volumes
Marcia Green is a witty Jewish political speechwriter who enjoys a passionate but unpromising live-in relationship with a dashing Irish coworker. Marcia's life is uncomplicated until she falls in love with the answer to her family's fervent prayers—a rich, handsome, well-educated Jewish lawyer. Some strong language and some explicit descriptions of sex. 1980.

The Stone Maiden   BR 4713
by Velda Johnston
2 volumes
A story of a young woman haunted by questions of her real identity. Her compulsive search leads her into a dangerous mystery of long-hidden Nazi treasure. She loses one love and gains another, as she follows a map pin-pointing the secret location of the treasure. 1980.

Maggie Craig   BR 5356
by Marie Joseph
2 volumes
A story of star-crossed love set amid the gloom and grime of turn-of-the-century Lancashire. Maggie Craig, the beautiful daughter of a country schoolmaster, is forced to earn her living in the cotton mills and obliged to pay for the rest of her life for the mistake of loving the wrong man. 1982.

These Tigers' Hearts   BR 4071
by Jane Land
2 volumes
An impoverished young Victorian Englishwoman, crossed in love by a rival, joins Miss Nightingale's school of nursing in London. Upon graduation she is employed by a Polish count to nurse his spoiled daughter. When the count nears death from an assassination attempt, the young woman nurses him back to health and wins his love. 1978.

Circle of Love   BR 4904
by Syrell Rogovin Leahy
2 volumes
The love story of Anna, a German Jew who was sent to live in France with a protective aunt during World War II, and Anton, a Polish survivor of a Nazi concentration camp. Searching for her parents after the war, she meets Anton when they both stumble upon the same abandoned farmhouse. The memorable three days they spend there comforting and loving each other haunt Anna even after she finds a comfortable life in the United States and a man who loves her. 1980.

A Key to Many Doors   BR 1956
by Emilie Loring
2 volumes
Almost resigned to her life as a spinster nurse, Nancy impulsively proposes to diplomat artist Peter Gerad. Trapped in a "marriage of convenience," she realizes that she is falling in love with him. 1967.

Look to the Stars   BR 1955
by Emilie Loring
2 volumes
A case of mistaken identity involves two girls, one from Boston's Back Bay society, the other from a modest background. Their lives touch when the handsome heir to a New England fortune meets and falls in love with one of them. 1960.

The Shining Years BR 1964
by Emilie Loring
3 volumes
A widow with a small son comes to stay with her brother-in-law at his castlelike home in Connecticut. While there she is attracted to a handsome major. 1972.

The Flowers of the Forest BR 4863
by Ruth Doan MacDougall
2 volumes
In 1878 Anne and Duncan, both poor Scottish immigrants, marry and move to New Hampshire to start the sheep farm Duncan yearns for. When hard times come upon them in 1901, they take in a schoolteacher as a boarder, and Anne, forty and the mother of six, falls in love with him. 1981.

Decision at Delphi BR 3021
by Helen MacInnes
5 volumes
On assignment to write a series on Mediterranean archaeological sites for a magazine, Ken discovers that his Greek-American photographer has disappeared, and he teams up with a pretty woman photographer. Strong language. 1960.

Miss Martha Mary Crawford BR 3208
by Catherine Marchant
3 volumes
Nineteenth-century English tale about a young woman who must help the family survive after her widowed father's death. She discovers that his money was squandered on a mistress,

but is given moral support by a young doctor. 1976.

Bid Time Return BR 2964
by Richard Matheson
3 volumes
A young man dying of a brain tumor falls in love with an actress who lived at the turn of the century and travels back into time to meet her. 1975.

The Jeweled Daughter BR 3202
by Anne Maybury
2 volumes
Set in Hong Kong where Sarah Brent, a jewel specialist, tries to acquire famous gems for a ruthless viscountess. Investigating a new acquisition that she suspects is stolen, Sarah runs into danger and her estranged husband. 1976.

The Thorn Birds BR 4284
by Colleen McCullough
3 volumes
Saga of the Cleary family set in a vast Australian sheep station. Central figures are beautiful Meggie and the only man she truly loves—handsome priest Ralph de Bricassart. Some strong language and some explicit descriptions of sex. Bestseller. 1977.

Dragon's Eye BR 3357
by Jennie Melville
2 volumes
Twelve years after she loses a stone castle on the island of Dragon's Eye to a rich man at an auction, actress Kate Melrose's dream comes true

when she finally inherits the estate. 1976.

The Sound of Waves   BR 3469
by Yukio Mishima
translated by Meredith Weatherby
2 volumes
The love story of Hatsue, a wealthy Japanese maiden trained to dive for precious pearls, and Shinji, a poor young fisherman. Relates the hazards that must be overcome before they marry. Some explicit descriptions of sex. 1971.

**My Friend Says It's Bullet-Proof
BR 1288**
by Penelope Mortimer
2 volumes
Muriel Rowbridge, a young English journalist, is sent by her editor on a public-relations mission to an un-named part of North America to help her recover from a breast cancer operation. On her journey she meets two men and falls in love with one. 1967.

Mary   BR 1480
by Vladimir Nabokov
translated by Michael Glenny in collaboration with the author
1 volume
A young officer exiled in Berlin discovers that his first love is leaving Russia to join her husband in Berlin. He begins a soul-searching debate with himself on whether or not he shall meet her secretly at the station. 1970.

Heaven and Hell and the Megas Factor   BR 2997
by Robert Nathan
1 volume
A gentle satirical fantasy about the state of the world. Sophia and Buckthorne, ambassadors from heaven and hell, respectively, are sent to earth to find a cure for man's increasing ills. The two spirit worlds are scandalized to discover their representatives have fallen in love. Some strong language. 1975.

The Last Station   BR 2058
by Bobby Jack Nelson
2 volumes
Attempting to ease the pain of an unhappy love affair, a young American seeks refuge on a cattle ranch in Australia's primitive outback area. Instead of peace, he finds himself embroiled in the affairs of the aborigines and involved with a young black girl who desires his love. Explicit descriptions of sex. 1972.

Kith   BR 3808
by P. H. Newby
2 volumes
Serving in 1941 as a private with the British medical corps in Cairo, David Cozens falls in love with his uncle's wife, an eighteen-year-old beauty who turns out to be a courtesan. Some explicit descriptions of sex. 1977.

The Sterile Cuckoo   BR 5138
by John Nichols
2 volumes
A rapturous, crazy love affair between an effervescent heroine and a fun-loving fraternity man who first meet in a bus station. Some strong language and descriptions of sex. 1965.

Miss Harriet Townshend   BR 4935
by Kathleen Norris
3 volumes
Centers on Miss Harriet Townshend, red-haired and Irish, a reigning belle, willing to fall in love. Her Spanish friend, widowed with three small sons, almost marries the wrong man—the one with whom Harriet finally falls in love. 1955.

The Eye of the Gods   BR 3969
by Richard Owen
2 volumes
Adventure and romance blossom in the Amazon jungle where an award-winning journalist and a determined woman paleontologist search for a legendary dinosaur. 1978.

The Moviegoer   BR 1854
by Walker Percy
2 volumes
Binx Bolling, a thoughtful young stockbroker working in New Orleans, falls in love with Kate Cutrer, whom he meets during the celebration of Mardi Gras. 1961.

Le Mans 24   BR 1807
by Denne Bart Petitclerc
2 volumes
At her first automobile race, Vali Beaufort sees her American lover, Chris, risk his life to win and watches a friend die in a fiery crash in the famous twenty-four-hour race in France. Terrified, she wonders whether she should marry Chris. 1971.

Carousel   BR 5327
by Rosamunde Pilcher
2 volumes
A contemporary romance set in a seaside town in Cornwall. While visiting a beloved aunt, Prue falls in love with the most interesting man she's ever met, an unpredictable artist who sowed many wild oats in his youth. Prue also forms an attachment to a poor-little-rich-girl who, she learns to her astonishment, is one of Daniel's wild oats. 1982.

The Empty House   BR 2793
by Rosamunde Pilcher
3 volumes
Virginia Keile, a wealthy young widow on vacation in England, meets the man she once loved as a girl. The meeting awakens feelings and memories of the past. 1975.

Snow in April   BR 3159
by Rosamunde Pilcher
2 volumes
In a borrowed car and a spring snowstorm, Jody and Caroline Cliburn set

out to search Scotland for their vanished brother, despite the fact that Caroline's wedding is only days away. 1972.

Who Were You with Last Night
BR 1909
by Frederic Raphael
2 volumes
Reluctantly settled into the routines of suburban domesticity and longing for his former freedom as part of the merchant marine, a man has an affair with an office colleague. 1971.

Summer of '42   BR 1656
by Herman Raucher
3 volumes
A middle-aged man returns to Packett Island off the New England coast and summons up memories of the summer of 1942 when he and his two buddies were fifteen. Preoccupied with sex, the three boys brooded, talked, read about it, and tried to turn theory into practice. Strong language. 1971.

A Georgian Love Story   BR 1732
by Ernest Raymond
4 volumes
In the London of the early years of George V's reign before World War I, a young journalist falls in love with a naive girl whose father runs a tobacco shop. 1971.

The Ballad of Kintillo   BR 3266
by Sally Rena
2 volumes
A young, idealistic Catholic priest

takes up his duties in Kintillo, Scotland. His friendship with a young woman grows to love and ends in tragedy. Some explicit descriptions of sex. 1975.

Love Play   BR 5000
by Rosemary Rogers
3 volumes
Sara agrees to masquerade as her actress sister to cover the sister's elopement. The elaborate ruse backfires when a tempestuous romance develops between Sara, still posing as her sister, and the arrogant Italian duke who is the obstacle to her sister's marriage. Some strong language and descriptions of sex. Bestseller. 1981.

Zandy's Bride   BR 2581
by Lillian Bos Ross
3 volumes
A rough pioneer from the primitive mountain country sends east for a mail order bride. She shares his harsh existence and teaches him how to love. 1969.

A Marriage of Convenience   BR 2020
by Elizabeth Rossiter
2 volumes
After her friend's sudden death, a widow with two young children marries her friend's husband and falls deeply in love with him. 1972.

Rhine Journey   BR 5096
by Ann Schlee
2 volumes
A nineteenth-century English spinster

taking a Rhine steamer trip with her relatives meets a man who reminds her of her one youthful love. The ensuing emotional tensions come into sharp contrast with her staid and melancholy existence, and she takes the first faltering steps to redefine her life and her relationships with others. 1980.

Love Story   BR 1688

by Erich Segal

1 volume

A rich Boston blue blood studying law at Harvard marries a Radcliffe music major of Italian descent against his family's wishes. Strong language. First part of a series. Followed by *Oliver's Story (BR 3549)*. Bestseller. 1970.

Oliver's Story   BR 3549

by Erich Segal

2 volumes

Two years after the death of his wife Jenny, Oliver Barrett III is still unable to come to terms with his guilt and grief. One day while jogging he meets a woman who attracts and mystifies him. He searches for his own identity through her. Second part of a series. Sequel to *Love Story (BR 1688)*. 1977.

The Doctor's Two Lives   BR 1373

by Elizabeth Seifert

3 volumes

The tensions and crises in the relationship of a dedicated young doctor and the girl he loves, who is being crowded out of his life. 1970.

The Cannaway Concern   BR 4707

by Graham Shelby

2 volumes

In eighteenth-century England, the young defiant daughter of Brydd and Elizabeth Cannaway elopes with courtly Brook Wintersill. She soon discovers that her life is endangered by his brutality and leaves for her parents' home, where Brook follows with his ruffian companions. Charlotte escapes once again and falls in love with Jacobite captain Matcham Lodge. Some violence and some strong language. Second part of series. Sequel to *The Cannaways (BRA 15765)*. 1980.

My Lady Hoyden   BR 5126

by Jane Sheridan

3 volumes

Set in the Victorian period. Follows the loves and fortunes of Amanda, a spirited beauty who earns a "reputation" after an innocent dalliance with the visiting Prince of Wales. Married to a grossly unsuitable blue blood, Amanda languishes until she falls in love with her dashing brother-in-law. 1981.

The Far Country   BR 3046

by Nevil Shute

3 volumes

Jennifer, an English doctor's daughter visiting cousins in Australia, falls in love with a Czech student who decides to accompany her when she returns to London. 1972.

Joy in the Morning   BR 1557
by Betty Smith
4 volumes
A woman marries a law student who is working his way through school, and the newlyweds face many difficulties—alienation from their parents, an unexpected baby, lack of money—but they find great joy in working through the hardships together. 1963.

Changes   BR 5556
by Danielle Steel
3 volumes
Melanie Adams seems to have it all: success as a TV documentary producer, twin teenage daughters, and a glamorous life that's perfect for a single mother. But Peter Hallam, a world-famous heart surgeon and widower with three children, makes her realize she doesn't have everything she wants. Some strong language and some descriptions of sex. Bestseller. 1983.

The Four Graces   BR 4494
By D. E. Stevenson
2 volumes
The four graces are the daughters of the village rector. The time is World War II, and the picture is of English men and women of all classes doing their bit to help keep life on an even keel. 1975.

Longsword   BR 5360
by Victoria Thorne
2 volumes
Young Gervase Escot, a medieval noble, is cheated out of his birthright by his jealous uncle. Fleeing from home disguised as a lowly scribe, Gervase ironically ends up in the service of the lady to whom he had been betrothed. 1982.

The Flowering   BR 2072
by Agnes Sligh Turnbull
2 volumes
Hester Carr, a widow in her thirties, yearns for a way of life aside from devotion to her cocker spaniel and music. Then John Justin comes to the suburb of Westbrook to write a book. 1972.

The Two Bishops   BR 4851
by Agnes Sligh Turnbull
3 volumes
Focuses on Cissie, a talented pianist, who enters into the lives of recently retired Bishop Ware and his successor Bishop Armstrong. Cissie lays seige to the young bishop's heart and helps him resolve the anguish of a private vow of celibacy. 1980.

The Death of Jim Loney   BR 4382
by James Welch
2 volumes
Solitary, brooding Jim Loney lives on the reservation in Harlem, Montana. Abandoned as a child by both his Indian mother and his reprobate white father, he wins the love of a rich

Texas girl who comes there to teach. His unrelenting path toward self-destruction halts their relationship. Some strong language and some explicit descriptions of sex. 1979.

Lost Island   BR 1448
by Phyllis A. Whitney
3 volumes
A woman returns to the small sea island of Hampton, Georgia, which she had left when she was seventeen after giving up her illegitimate child fathered by her youthful lover. But instead of exorcising the "old nostalgic magic" of her home, her visit brings the two old lovers back together. 1970.

Poinciana   BR 4708
by Phyllis A. Whitney
3 volumes
Shy, timid Sharon Hollis, daughter of a famous international chanteuse and her glamorous manager, agrees to marry wealthy, sixty-year-old Ross Logan when Sharon's parents are killed in a Belfast bombing. Depressing surprises, however, await at Poinciana, their fabulous Palm Beach estate. 1980.

The Lover   BR 3954
by Abraham B. Yehoshua
translated by Philip Simpson
4 volumes
Adam is obsessed with finding the young and mysterious Gabriel, his wife's lover, who disappeared during Israel's Yom Kippur War in 1973. An intense novel that probes the complexities of love. Some strong language and some explicit descriptions of sex. 1977.

Bibliographies

Bibliographies of books on disc and cassette and in braille are available on request from network libraries. They cover a variety of subjects and are produced in large-print, disc, and braille formats. Some bibliographies may no longer be available in all formats.

Bestsellers
Lists bestselling fiction of the twentieth century. Published in 1979.

Biography—The Arts
Guide to biographies and autobiographies of people in the arts. Published in 1980.

Biography—Government and Politics
Guide to biographies and autobiographies of people in government and politics at home and abroad. Published in 1980.

Health
Emphasizes the human body, physical health care, and medical history and research. Published in 1979.

Historical Fiction
Books featuring the events and people of history through fiction. Published in 1983.

Home Management
Books on the many aspects of the home including cooking, gardening, child care, and finance. Published in 1977.

Mysteries
Works of detective and mystery fiction. Published in 1982.

Religion
Sacred writings and books on religions around the world and other inspirational subjects. Published in 1979.

Science
Books on botany, astronomy, physics, and many other scientific and technological areas. Published in 1978.

Science Fiction
Full-length novels and anthologies of short stories about speculative ideas, marvelous discoveries, and travel and adventures in time and space. Published in 1979.

Sports
Books about sports, outdoor activities, and sportswriters on sports. Published in 1977.

Westerns
Stories about the West and the American frontier. Published in 1983.

Young Adult Fiction
Books for readers in the twelve-to-twenty age group. Published in 1981.

Discs

Index Discs

Cassettes

A

Index Cassettes

Index Cassettes

Q, R

Index Cassettes

Index Cassettes

Braille

Index Braille

Index Braille

☆ U.S. GOVERNMENT PRINTING OFFICE: 1984-449-782